FASHION CROCHET

Fashion Crochet

BY
Caroline Horne

HEARTHSIDE PRESS INC.

Publishers • **New York**

British Edition First Published 1969 by Mills & Boon Limited
Copyright © 1969, 1970 by Caroline Horne
Library of Congress Catalog Card Number 77-130537
ISBN 0-8208-0335-9
American Edition First Published 1970 by Hearthside Press Inc.

Contents

Acknowledgements

The revisions for the American edition were edited by the Coats and Clark Design Studio.

The stitches were taken, with permission, from the Coats Sewing Group Book *Crochet Stitches*.

The fashion drawings are by Yvonne Jones.

Photographs by Gordon Crocker.

Note

The yarns given for the various patterns were still in circulation when this book went to press; the manufacturer however, may decide to withdraw certain colors at any time.

Substitute yarns, although of the same type and ply will vary, for each manufacturer's brand is slightly different, and different textures will result because of this.

So, it is most important that before each garment is started, a trial pattern piece be made to test gauge and "feel".

Introduction

As a teacher of Fashion Crochet I have often been asked the question 'Is it very difficult?' The answer is simple: 'No it isn't!' But once you have mastered the art of holding the crochet hook and the few stitches that there are in *Fashion Crochet*, everything else begins to fall into place. Soon you will find yourself making attractive chic clothes—a welcome addition to any wardrobe—at a fraction of the price that they would cost in the shops, with the added incentive of being able to have exactly the right color and shape that you want when you want it. Anyone can do Fashion Crochet and there is no time like the present for embarking on this absorbing, creative and constructive craft which is currently enjoying such a vogue in the world of fashion.

Abbreviations

ch.=chain
f. ch.=foundation chain
ch. grp.=chain group
st.=stitch
sl. st.=slip stitch
sc.=single crochet

dc.=double crochet
dbl.=double
dc. grp.=double crochet group
dc. row=double crochet row
hlf. dc. or h. dc.=half double crochet
tr.=treble
blk.=block
sp.=space
beg.=beginning
inc.=increase
dec.=decrease
grp.=group
hlf. grp.=half group
y.o.h.=yarn over hook
*=repeat
( )=repeat what is in ( ) the number of times specified

HOW TO LEARN CROCHET

Fig. 1   How to make a Slip loop.

Start by making a slip loop with the yarn as in fig 1. Then:
1. Hold loop in place between thumb and forefinger of left hand. With right hand, take hold of broad bar of hook as you would a pencil. Insert your hook through loop with right hand.

Single crochet (Sc.)

Double crochet (Dc.)

2. Now pull short end of yarn and ball in opposite directions to bring loop close around the end of the hook, but not too tightly.

3. Hold the hook with the loop on, between the thumb and forefinger of the left hand, pass yarn over the first 3 fingers and under and then over the little finger of the left hand. Now gently pull yarn so that it lies over and around your fingers firmly but not tightly. Transfer hook into your right hand, holding knot of loop between the thumb and forefinger of the left hand. Take hold of the broad bar of hook in right hand as you would a pencil and bring middle finger forward to rest near tip of hook.

The stitches

Chain stitch (ch.) This is the basic stitch for all crochet work. Adjust fingers of left hand as in fig 2.

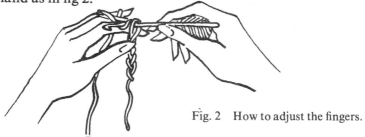

Fig. 2   How to adjust the fingers.

The middle finger is raised to regulate the tension while the 3rd and little fingers prevent the yarn from running too freely. The motion of the hook in the right hand and the yarn in the left hand should be coordinated. T will come with practice.

Now with hands and yarn in position, pass your hook under and catch yarn with hook (fig 3), drawing it through loop on hook (fig 4).

Repeat this step until you have the required number of ch. st.

Keep the thumb and forefinger of your left hand near the st. on which you are working.

The suppleness of the wrists plays a part in crochet; two of the faults that newcomers to crochet make are to work either too tightly or too loosely. Don't let this worry you. Try to relax your hands and wrists. Ease, together with an even tension will come with practice.

Work a practice ch. until you have an even tension.

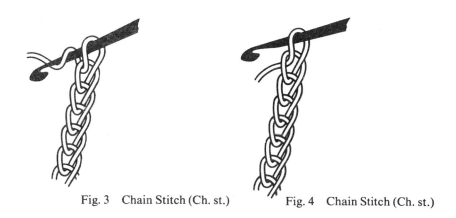

Fig. 3   Chain Stitch (Ch. st.)   Fig. 4   Chain Stitch (Ch. st.)

Slip stitch (sl. st.) This is used when an invisible st. is required. Good examples of this are the armholes and the shaping of the shoulders.
Insert hook into the 2 top threads of st. Y.o.h. and with one motion draw through st. and loop on hook; 1 loop remains on hook.
Note: It is usual in all crochet to pick up the 2 top threads of each st. unless otherwise stated.

Fig. 5   Slip Stitch (Sl. st.)

Single Crochet (sc.) This st. makes a firm fabric which is attractive for a suit and also effective for borders on sweaters and cardigans.
Make a ch. of 20 for a practice piece.

1st row

1. Insert hook from the front under the 2 top threads of 2nd ch. from hook.

2. Catch yarn with hook (fig 6) and draw through ch. There are now 2 loops on hook (fig 7).

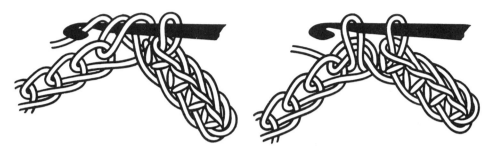

Fig. 6   Single Crochet (Sc.)   Fig. 7   Single Crochet (Sc.)

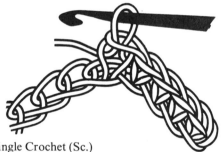

Fig. 8   Single Crochet (Sc.)

3. Y.o.h. and draw through 2 loops; 1 loop remains on hook (fig 8).

4. For next sc. insert hook under 2 threads of next ch. and **repeat** steps 2 and 3.

5. **Repeat** step 4 until you have an sc. in each st. At the end of the row, work 1 ch. to turn. This enables you to turn your work easily. Now turn your work with the reverse side facing you.

2nd row

1. Insert hook under 2 top threads of the 1st st. (the last stitch made on the previous row).

2. Y.o.h. and draw through st.; 2 loops on hook.

3. Y.o.h. and draw through 2 loops; 1 loop on hook.

4. For next sc. insert hook under the 2 top threads of next st. and **repeat** steps 2 and 3.

Repeat step 4 until you have worked a sc. into every st.; 1 ch. Turn.

The 1 turning ch. of each row is **not** counted as a st. in the following row.

Repeat this row until you have become familiar with the st. Fasten-off.

How to fasten-off

Omit the turning ch. at the end of last row, cut yarn a few inches from work, bring loose end through the loop on hook and pull tightly.

Half Double Crochet (hlf. dc.) makes an attractive firm fabric, and is a favorite of mine for children's clothes.

Make 20 ch. for a practice piece.

1st row

1. Y.o.h. (fig 9) insert hook from the front under 2 top threads of 3rd ch. from hook.

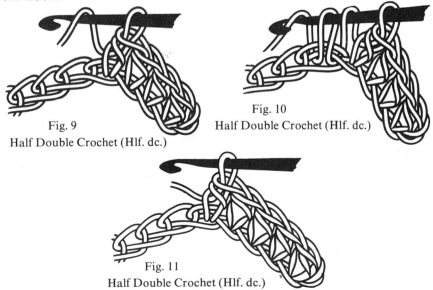

Fig. 9
Half Double Crochet (Hlf. dc.)

Fig. 10
Half Double Crochet (Hlf. dc.)

Fig. 11
Half Double Crochet (Hlf. dc.)

2. Y. o. h. and pull loop through ch., 3 loops on hook, y. o. h. (fig 10) draw through all loops on hook, 1 loop remains on hook (fig 11). A hlf. dc. is now completed.

3. For next hlf. dc., y.o.h. Insert hook under the 2 top threads of next ch.

4. **Repeat** steps 2 and 3 until 1 hlf. dc. has been made in each ch. At the end of the row make 2 ch. Turn.

2nd row

1. Y.o.h. Insert hook under the 2 top threads of 1st st., i.e. the last st. on previous row.

2. Y.o.h. and pull through st. There are now 3 loops on hook, y.o.h. and draw through all loops on hook.

3. For next hlf. dc., y.o.h., insert hook under the 2 top threads of next st. and **repeat** step 2.

4. **Repeat** steps 3 and 2 until 1 hlf. dc. has been made in each st., 2 ch. Turn.

Note: The 2 ch. turning st. of each row does not count as a st. on the following rows.

Double Crochet (dc.) is the most popular st. in crochet because so many different designs can be made from it.

Make a practice piece of 20 ch.

1st row

1. Y.o.h. (fig 12) insert hook under the 2 top threads of the 4th ch. from hook.

2. Y.o.h. and draw through st. There are now 3 loops on hook (fig 13).

3. Y.o.h. and draw through 2 loops, 2 loops remain on hook (fig 14).

4. Y.o.h. again and draw through 2 remaining loops; 1 loop remains on hook (fig 15). 1 dc. is now completed.

5. For next dc., y.o.h., insert hook under 2 top threads of next ch. and **repeat** steps 2—5 until 1 dc. has been made in each ch.

6. At the end of the row, work 3 ch. Turn.

Note: Turning ch. here counts as the 1st dc. on next and every following row, therefore the 1st dc. of each row is always skipped.

Fig. 12   Double Crochet (Dc.)

Fig. 13   Double Crochet (Dc.)

Fig. 14   Double Crochet (Dc.)

Fig. 15   Double Crochet (Dc.)

Fig. 16   Treble (Tr.)

2nd row

1. Y.o.h. insert hook under the 2 top threads of the 5th st. from the hook (the 2nd dc. of previous row).

Repeat steps 2—6 of 1st row.

Repeat the 2nd row until you are familiar with st. Fasten-off.

Treble (tr.) This is a st. which is rarely used by itself, though one can make most attractive designs combining it with other basic sts.

Make a practice ch. of 20.

1st row

1. Y.o.h. 2 times and insert hook under the 2 top threads of the 5th ch. from hook.

2. Y.o.h. and draw through the ch. There are now 4 loops on the hook (fig 16).

3. Y.o.h. again and draw through 2 loops (3 loops remain on hook).

4. Y.o.h. and draw through 2 loops (2 loops remain on hook).

5. Y.o.h. once again and draw through the remaining 2 loops (1 loop remains on hook).

6. For the next tr., y. o. h. 2 times and insert hook under the 2 top threads of next ch. **Repeat** steps 2—6 until 1 tr. has been made in each ch.

7. At the end of the row make 4 ch. and turn. The turning 4 ch. counts as the 1st tr. on the next row and every following row, therefore the 1st tr. is always skipped.

2nd row

1. Insert hook under the 2 top threads of the 6th st. from hook (2nd st. on previous row).

2. **Repeat** steps 2—7 on 1st row.

Repeat 2nd row until you are familiar with this st. Fasten-off.

Turning at ends of rows

A certain number of ch. are worked at the end of each row to bring work into position for the next row. The number of turning ch. required is always dependant on the st. that you intend to begin the next row with.

Sc.
1 ch. to turn.

Hlf. dc.
2 ch. to turn.

Dc.
3 ch. to turn.

Tr.
4 ch. to turn.

How to Decrease in Crochet

Sc.
Work off 2 sc. thus: Insert hook into next sc. and pull loop through. Insert hook into the following sc.—pull loop through (3 loops on hook) y.o.h. and draw through all loops on hook.

Hlf. dc.
Work off 2 hlf. dc. as 1 hlf. dc. thus: * Y.o.h. draw a loop through next hlf. dc. **Repeat** from * once more (5 loops on hook) y.o.h. and draw through all loops on hook.

Dc.
Work off 2 dc. as 1 dc. thus: Y.o.h. draw a loop through next dc. (3 loops on hook) y.o.h. and draw through 2 loops (2 loops on hook). Y.o.h. draw a loop through next dc. (4 loops on hook) y.o.h. and draw through 2 loops (3 loops on hook) y.o.h. and draw through all loops on hook.

Inc.
By working 2 sts. into 1 st.

Gauge or tension

This means the number of sts. per inch and the number of rows per inch. The gauge is most important but it is something which can always be adjusted quite easily. Before starting a garment always work a 3 in. sample square of the pattern. Pin this down onto a cloth and mark off with pins a 2 in. measurement in the center of the square and see if the gauge corresponds with the directions in the pattern. If you have more rows and sts., use a larger size hook. Should you have fewer rows and sts. use a smaller-size hook. An even gauge should be achieved if you hold your work firmly in the left hand with the yarn running freely. Try to keep the right hand and wrist relaxed and supple. Do not be discouraged if you do not achieve an even gauge at first. This will come with practice. However do **not** begin your garment until your gauge corresponds with the directions in the pattern.

Yarns and hook

Crochet gives a firm fabric in any type of yarn and never before has there been such a variety available, both in type and color. For an easy-to-work yarn suitable for a beginner, a yarn with a firm twist is excellent. This if used with a smooth hook with a narrow rounded end enables beginners to crochet without any difficulties.

Joining of yarn

Knots must never be used. If 3 or 4 ply yarn is being used, thread the new ball of yarn into a darning needle and weave it through the end of the yarn just used for about 3 ins. Smooth it out between thumb and finger and cut off loose ends of yarn. If thicker yarn is being used, either join at the end of a row or unravel the ends for about 4—5 ins., cut away 1 strand from each end of the yarn and twist the remaining strands together. Cut away loose ends.

Measuring

Work must always be measured on the straight of a garment. The depth of the armhole is measured on the straight from the 1st row of the dec. Do not rely altogether on the tape measure or ruler. With crochet one must also count. It has been said "If you can count, you can crochet", so do remember to count the rows or patterns on pieces that are to be joined together and work exactly the same number on each one, e.g. the back and the front of a skirt.

Fastening-off in crochet

Break off yarn, leaving sufficient to weave in, then draw the end of the yarn through the loop, pulling tightly.

Pressing

This must be done with great care. You can spoil a garment by over-pressing. Each piece should be pressed separately before sewing-up, so with the wrong side of the fabric facing, smooth out onto a padded surface and place pins all around the edges. Measure up, down and across to ensure that you have the correct size, taking care to keep the rows or patterns straight. I like to use a steam iron for pressing crochet garments. Just skim over the surface of the fabric without actually touching it. However if a steam iron is not available use a damp cloth, a fairly hot iron and, most essential of all a light hand. This is particularly true if crepe has been used as over-pressing spoils the appearance of this beautifully finished fabric. Do not remove the pins from the blocked pieces until the pieces are fully dry.

Man-made yarns such as Nylon, Wintuk,[*]etc.

The manufacturers of these yarns stipulate that pressing is not necessary, but my own personal views are that a very light pressing will enhance the appearance of the finished garment.

Making-up a garment

This, in my opinion depends on the pattern used in the garment. With most patterns, however, I prefer to crochet the edges together with an sc. st. as this gives a much neater finish. Alternatively sew the edges together with a fine back st., as close to the edge as possible. Whichever method is used, pin the edges together, making sure that rows or patterns match exactly. If the sc. method is being used and the original yarn is of a coarse texture, use a matching one in a finer ply. If the original yarn is a crepe and the sewing method is being used, this can be easily split into separate strands and used, thus resulting in an excellent fine seam. When joining the shoulders, take the line of stitching straight across the shapings. Press each seam as it is joined. Sc. borders must be sewn together using a flat seam.

Finishing a skirt waistline

Cut 1 inch wide elastic to fit waist and join into a circle. Pin elastic to skirt waist distributing fullness evenly all around. Using yarn, and having the elastic stretched slightly over the 1st finger, sew with a herringbone st. catching the elastic top and bottom.

READING PATTERNS

Learning to read a pattern is essential. Before beginning any of the garments practice these simple designs and make yourself familiar with pattern reading.

Pattern 1

This is suitable for the hemline of a crochet dress (the dress being perfectly plain would be worked with 1 row dc. and 1 row sc.). Make 40 ch.

1st row (right side)
1 dc. into the 4th ch. from hook, 1 dc. into each of the next 36 ch., 1 ch. Turn.

2nd row
1 sc. into each dc., ending with 1 sc. into turning ch. of 1st row, 3 ch. Turn.

3rd row
Skip the 1st sc., 1 dc. into each sc. to end, 1 ch. Turn.

4th row
As 2nd row.

5th row
Skip 2 sc. (2 dc., 2 ch., 2 dc.) into next sc. * skip 3 sc. (2 dc., 2 ch., 2 dc.) into next sc. **Repeat** from * ending with skip 1 sc., 1 dc. into last sc., 3 ch. Turn.

6th row
* (2 dc., 2 ch., 2 dc.) into next 2 ch. sp. **Repeat** from * ending with 1 dc. into turning ch., 3 ch. Turn.

7th, 8th, 9th, 10th, 11th rows
Repeat row 6, omitting the turning ch. on last row.

12th row
1 ch., 1 sc. into each dc., 1 sc. into turning ch., 3 ch. Turn.
Work rows 3 and 4 alternately, 3 times. Fasten-off.

Pattern no. 1   View of enlarged st.

Border

Turn to lower edge of work and with right side facing, attach yarn and work 1 sc. into each f.ch. Fasten-off.

Pattern 2

Is a st. which is suitable for a sweater or a dress; it has a picot border. Make 37 ch.

1st row
1 dc. into the 4th ch. from hook, * skip 2 ch., and work 1 sc. and 2 dc. into next ch. **Repeat** from * to end of row (12 grps.) 3 ch. Turn.

2nd row
1 dc. into 1st dc. of 1st grp. * 1 sc., 2 dc. into 1st dc. of next grp. **Repeat** from * to end of row, 3 ch. Turn. (This row forms the pattern.) **Repeat** this row 14 times more. Fasten-off.

Border

Turn work to lower edge and with wrong side facing, rejoin yarn and work 3 sc. into each f. ch. in which a grp. is worked. Turn.

Picot edge

* 3 ch., 1 sc. into 3rd ch. from hook, skip 2 sc., 1 sl. st. into next sc. **Repeat** from * to end. Fasten-off.

Pattern 3

This trim could be attached to the neck of a plain dress or around the neckline and lower edge of a knitted sweater and will greatly enhance the look of the garment. It can also be used as a trim for a lampshade, perhaps worked in gold thread, turning the lampshade into something really rather special.
Start by making a ch. of the desired length.

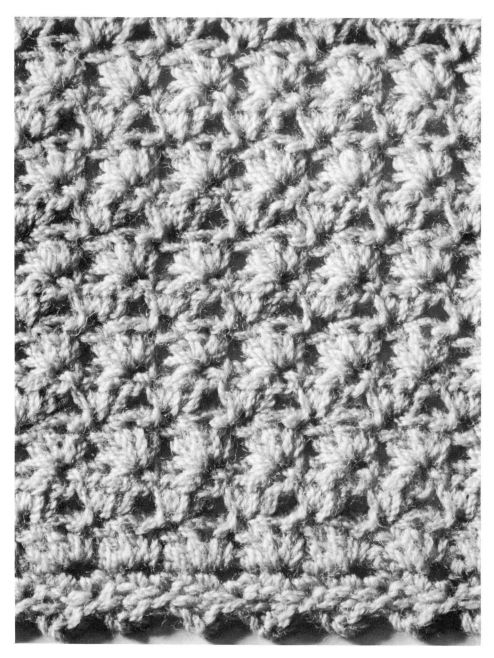

Pattern no. 2   with picot border (lower edge) View of enlarged st.

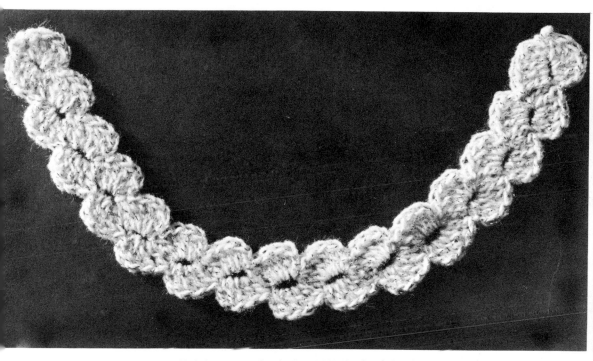

Pattern no. 3   "This is how the fabric should look after it has been crocheted."

1st row

1 sc. into 3rd ch. from hook, 1 ch., 4 dc. into same ch., * skip 3 ch., 1 sc., 1 ch., 4 dc. (shell) into next ch. **Repeat** from * ending with 1 sc. into last ch., 3 ch. Turn.
Turn work upside down.

2nd row

Working along f. ch., 1 sc., 1 ch., 4 dc. into the same ch. where last shell was worked in the 1st row, * skip 3 ch., (1 sc., 1 ch., 4 dc.) into next ch. in which shell has been worked. **Repeat** from * ending with 1 sl. st. into turning ch. of 1st row. Fasten-off.

Pattern 4

Is worked in motifs in 2 shades of color (light and dark); it makes a good 'filler' for that low-necked dress which we sometimes feel is just that little bit too low.

Motif

Using dark yarn, make 6 ch. and join into a ring with a sl. st.

1st round
Work 15 sc. into ring, join with a sl. st. Break off yarn.

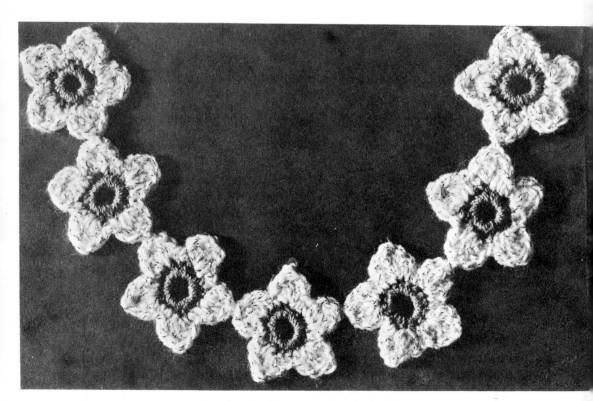

Pattern no. 4   "This is how the fabric should look after it has been crocheted."

2nd round

Join in light yarn and work * 1 sc. into next sc., 2 dc., 1 tr., 2 dc. into next sc., 1 sc. into next sc. **Repeat** from * all around and join with a sl. st. (5 petals). Fasten-off.

When the required number of motifs have been made, sew together as illustrated.

How to make
a Handbag

Materials

Rug Yarn (70-yd. skeins) = 4 skeins; plastic or bone hook, size H; ½ yd. material for lining; ½ yard semi-stiff interlining, if desired; handbag frame.

Gauge
3 grps. = 2 inches; 2 rows = 1½ inches

Measurement
10 inches by 8 inches

Method

Make 34 ch. to measure 11 ins.

1st row

Y. o. h., insert hook into 2nd ch. from hook and pull loop through, 2 times, y. o. h., skip 1 ch., insert hook into next ch. and pull loop through. Y. o. h. and draw through all loops on hook, 1 ch. (1 grp. made)* (y.o.h., insert hook into same ch. where last loop was pulled up, and pull loop through), 2 times, y. o. h., skip 1 ch., insert hook into next ch. and pull loop through. Y. o. h. and draw through all loops on hook, 1 ch.
Repeat from * to end of row, 16 grps., 1 ch. Turn.

2nd row

Y. o. h., insert hook into 1st ch. preceding 1st grp., draw loop through, 2 times, y. o. h., insert hook into the st. at top of next grp. (grp. st.) draw loop through. Y. o. h. and draw through all loops on hook, 1 ch. * (y. o. h., insert hook into the top of same grp. st. and draw loop through), 2 times, y. o. h., insert hook into next grp. st. and draw loop through. Y. o. h. and draw through all loops on hook, 1 ch. **Repeat** from * ending (y. o. h., insert hook into the top of same grp. st.), 2 times. Y. o. h., insert hook into turning ch. of previous row, draw loop through. Y. o. h., and draw through all loops on hook, 16 grps., 1 ch. Turn.
Repeat the 2nd row until 11 rows have been worked.

12th row

2 ch., 1 sc. into every st. (32 sc.) Do not turn: 2 ch. Working left to right, 1 sc. into each sc. Fasten-off. Turn work upside down. Join yarn to starting point of ch.

then:

1st row

1 ch. (y.o.h., insert hook into same ch. and draw loop through), 2 times y. o. h., skip 1 ch., insert hook into next ch. Draw loop through,

y.o.h. and draw through all loops on hook, 1 ch. * (Y.o.h., insert hook into same ch., draw loop through), 2 times, y.o.h., skip 1 ch., insert hook into next ch. and draw loop through. Y.o.h. and draw through all loops on hook, 1 ch. **Repeat** from * to end of row, 1 ch. Turn. **Repeat** 2nd row of pattern until 11 rows have been completed and finish as for 1st side.

Gussets

Make 2. Commence with 8 ch.
Work in pattern as before (3 grps.) for 3 rows. Inc. 1 grp. in next row between 2nd and 3rd grps. Work 3 rows more, Inc. 1 grp. in center of next row. Work 2 rows straight. (10 rows in gusset.) Fasten-off.

Making-up

Press each piece very lightly, join gussets to sides—(gussets should reach up to the bottom of the 1st row from top of sides.) Cut lining 12 ins. wide by 15 ins. deep. Lining should only come up to top of gussets. Thread rods of frame through the ch. st. at the bottom of the 11th row. The hinges of the frame should fall outside the gussets.

SUGGESTED COLORS
Fudge Brown
Black

How to make Crochet Pants

Materials

Directions are given for Size 10. Changes for Sizes 12, 14 and 16 are in parentheses.

WINTUK *sport yarn, 2 ply (2 oz. skeins): 18 (20, 22, 24) ounces of Evening Violet; crochet hook, size H; **skirt or neck zipper,** 9-inch length; hook and eye; ribbon for waistband.

GAUGE: 5 sts. (3 sc. with 2 ch.-1 sps. between) = 1 inch; 5 rows = 1 inch. Be sure to check your gauge before starting garment. Use any size hook which will obtain the stitch gauge above.

BLOCKING MEASUREMENTS

SIZES	10	12	14	16
Body Waist Size (In Inches)	24	25½	27	29
Hip	34½	36	38	40
Actual Crocheting Measurements				
Waist	24	25½	27	29
Length from waist to lower edge of leg				
	38	38½	39	40

* Red Heart

Method

RIGHT BACK LEG Starting at lower edge, make a chain of 56 (58, 60, 62) sts., having 5 ch. sts. to 1 inch.

Foundation row: Sc. in 2nd ch. from hook, * ch. 1 skip next ch., sc. in next ch. Repeat from * across. There are 55 (57, 59, 61) sts. or 28 (29, 30, 31) sc. with 27 (28, 29, 30) ch.-1 sps. between. Ch. 1, turn. Now work in pattern as follows: **1st row:** Sc. in first sc., sc. in first sp., * ch. 1, sc. in next sp. Repeat from * across to within last sc., sc. in last sc. Ch. 1, turn. **2nd row:** Sc. in first sc., * ch. 1, sc. in next sp. Repeat from * across to within last 2 sc., ch. 1, skip next sc., sc. in last sc. Ch. 1, turn. There are the same number of sts. as on foundation row. Repeat last 2 rows for pattern. Work even in pattern until total length is 22 (22, 22½, 22½) inches, ending with 2nd row. Place a marker in last st. worked to indicate crotch edge. Ch. 1, turn. Now inc. at crotch edge as follows: **1st inc. row:** Sc. in first sc., ch. 1, sc. in first sp., * ch. 1, sc. in next sp. Repeat from * across to within last sc., sc. in last sc. Ch. 1, turn. **2nd inc. row:** Work same as 2nd pattern row to within last sc., ch. 1, sc. in last sc. There is one ch.-1 sp. and one sc. more than on previous 2nd pattern row. Ch. 1, turn. **Next 4 rows:** Work even in pattern. **Following 8 rows:** Repeat last 6 rows once more, then repeat first and 2nd inc. rows once. There are 61 (63, 65, 67) sts. on last row. Work even until total length is 26 (26, 26½, 26½) inches, ending at crotch edge and omitting turning chain at end of last row. Turn.

Crotch Shaping: 1st dec. row: *Sl. st. in first sc. and in next ch.—2 sts. decreased;* ch. 1, sc. in next sc., sc. in next sp. and complete as for first pattern row. **2nd row:** Work in pattern across, omitting turning chain. There is 1 sc. and 1 sp. less than on previous 2nd pattern row. **3rd through 12th rows:** Repeat last 2 rows 5 times. At end of last row ch. 1, turn. Now dec. 2 sts. at crotch edge every inch 2 times in all. Work even in pattern over remaining 45 (47, 49, 51) sts. until length from first row of crotch shaping is 7 (7½, 7½, 7½) inches, ending at crotch edge.

First Dart Panel: 1st row: Sc. in first sc., sc. in next sp., (ch. 1, sc. in next sp.) 8 (9, 9, 10) times; sc. in next sc. Mark last st. worked to indicate dart edge. Do not work over remaining sts. Ch. 1, turn. Continue over this set of 19 (21, 21, 23) sts. only. **2nd row:** Work in pattern across. Ch. 1, turn. **3rd row:** *Draw up a loop in each of first 2 sts., yarn over and draw through all 3 loops on hook*—**one st. decreased:** * ch. 1, sc. in next sp. Repeat from * across to within last sc., sc. in last sc. Ch. 1, turn. **4th, 5th and 6th rows:** Sc. in first sc., * ch. 1, sc. in next sp. Repeat from * across to within last st., sc. in last st. Ch. 1, turn. **7th row:** Dec. one st. over first 2 sts.—crotch edge; sc. in next sp., * ch. 1, sc. in next sp. Repeat from * across to within last 3 sts., ch. 1, skip next sc., *dec. one st. over last 2 sts.*—**one st. decreased at dart edge.** Ch. 1, turn. **8th, 9th and 10th rows:** Repeat first pattern row, ending with ch. 1, skip next sc., sc. in last sc. Ch. 1, turn. **Next 4 rows:** Being careful to keep in pattern, dec. one st. at crotch edge on next row, then work 3 rows even. **Following 4 rows:** Dec. one st. at both ends of next row, then work 3 rows even. **19th row:** Dec. one st. at crotch edge, work in pattern across—there remain 12 (14, 14, 16) sts. Work even in pattern until length from first row of crotch shaping is 12 (12½, 12½, 13½) inches. Break off and fasten.

Center Panel: 1st row: Attach yarn to the sp. following marked st. at dart edge on last long row, ch. 1, sc. in same sp., (ch. 1, sc. in next sp.) 6 times; For Sizes 14 and 16 Only: sc. in next sc. **For All Sizes:** Do not work over remaining sts. Ch. 1, turn. Working over these 13 (13, 14, 14) sts. only and being careful to keep in pattern, dec. one st. at both ends every 2 inches 2 times in all. Work even over remaining 9 (9, 10, 10) sts. until panel measures same as previous panel. Break off and fasten.

Second Dart Panel: 1st row: Attach yarn to next st. following Center Panel on last long row, ch. 1, sc. in same place and work in pattern to end of row. Being careful to keep in pattern, work same as Center Panel.

LEFT BACK LEG Work same as Right Back Leg.

RIGHT FRONT LEG Starting at lower edge, make a chain of 56 (58, 60, 62) sts., having 5 ch. sts. to 1 inch. Work even in pattern as for Right Back Leg over 55 (57, 59, 61) sts. until total length is 26½ (27, 27, 27½) inches, ending with 2nd pattern row. Place a marker in last st. worked to indicate crotch edge.

Crotch Shaping: At crotch edge, dec. 2 sts. at beg. of next row and every other row thereafter until 49 (51, 53, 55) sts. remain, then dec. one st. at crotch edge every other row until 39 (41, 43, 45) sts. remain.

Work even until length from first row of crotch shaping is 7½ inches, ending at side edge. Dec. one st. at side edge on next row and on the following 3rd row. Work even over remaining 37 (39, 41, 43) sts. until length from first row of crotch shaping is 8½ (8½, 9, 9½) inches, ending at crotch edge.

First Dart Panel: 1st row: Sc. in first sc., sc. in next sp., (ch. 1, sc. in next sp.) 6 (7, 8, 9) times; sc. in next sc. Mark last st. worked to indicate dart edge. Do not work over remaining sts. Ch. 1, turn. Working over this set of 15 (17, 19, 21) sts. only, dec. one st. at dart edge when length of panel is about 1½ inches. Work even for 1 inch, then dec. one st. at same edge on next row. Work even over 13 (15, 17, 19) sts. until length from first row of crotch shaping is 11½ (11½, 12, 12½) inches. Break off and fasten.

Center Panel: Attach yarn to the sp. following marked st. at dart edge on last long row, ch. 1, sc. in same sp., (ch. 1, sc. in next sp.) 5 times. Working over these 11 sts. only, dec. one st. at both ends when length of panel is 1½ inches. Work even for 1 inch then dec. one st. at both ends of next row. Work even over remaining 7 sts. until panel measures same as previous panel.

Second Dart Panel: Working over the remaining 11 sts. of last long row, dec. one st. at dart edge when length is 1½ inches. Work even for 1 inch, then dec. one st. at same edge on next row. Working even over 9 sts., complete as for previous panel.

LEFT FRONT LEG Work same as Right Front Leg. Block to measurements. Sew darts. Sew center front and back seams, inner leg seams and right side seam. Sew left side seam to within 8 inches of waist for zipper opening.

Waistband: 1st row: With right side facing, attach yarn to top of zipper opening, ch. 1, sc. evenly across waist edge, holding in to fit. Ch. 1, turn. **Next 6 rows:** Sc. in each sc. across. Ch. 1, turn. Do not turn at end of last row; sc. evenly along both edges of zipper opening. Break off and fasten.

Edgings: 1st rnd: Working along opposite side of starting chain, attach yarn to inner seam at lower edge of a leg, ch. 1, sc. in each ch. around. Join with sl. st. to first sc. **Next 3 rnds:** Ch. 1, sc. in each sc. around. Join. Turn at end of last rnd. **Last rnd:** Sl. st. loosely in each sc. around. Join. Break off and fasten. Sew in zipper. Sew ribbon to inside of waistband. Sew hook and eye to top of zipper opening. If desired, line pants.

How to make a Crochet Hat

Materials

"Speed-Cro-Sheen" Mercerized Cotton = 5 balls; steel hook No. 1/0 (zero); buckram or net hat shape (obtainable from any good millinery supply store).

Measurement
To fit a small head.

Method

Commence with a ch. approx. 6½ yds. long.

1st row
1 dc. into the 8th ch. from hook, * 2 ch., skip 2 ch., 1 dc. into next ch.
Repeat from * to end.
Note: If you work loosely . . . you will get a better finish for your hat by
working thus: in the 1st row—1 dc. into the 5th ch. from hook, * 1 ch.,
skip 1 ch., 1 dc. into the next ch. **Repeat** from * to end.
Your work now looks like a ladder, work over each rung or dc. bar.
thus: Ch. 3, 6 dc. over the 1st rung (dc. bar.) Turn. * 6 dc. over the next
rung. Turn. **Repeat** from * to end. This forms a zigzag pattern.

Making-up

Beginning at center of crown of hat shape, sew frilling in rounds stitching frilling together as you work. Finish hat off by lining it.
Note: This hat can also be made with 2 strands of J. & P. Coats' "Knit-
Cro-Sheen" of which there are many shades to choose from. This is also
very effective worked in a No. 20 crochet cotton used double throughout, working 6 tr. over the dc. bar instead of 6 dc. Use a No. 2 steel
crochet hook.

SUGGESTED COLORS
White
Black
Spanish Red
Hunter's Green
Blue Sparkle
Nu-Ecru

How to make a pair of Stockings

Materials

WINTUK * Sock & Sweater Yarn, 3 ply (2 oz. skeins), 8 ounces; steel hooks No. 1 and No. 2.

* Red Heart

Gauge
5 grps. to 2 inches, 7 rows to 2 inches over pattern, using No. 1 hook.

Measurements
Leg from top to bottom of heel—28½ inches
Length of foot—9½ inches (measurements adjustable)

Method

With No. 2 hook, begin with the ribbing by making 11 ch.

1st row
1 sc. into 2nd ch. from hook, 1 sc. into each ch. to end. 1 ch. Turn.

2nd row
Working into back of st. only, 1 sc. into each st. to end, 1 ch. Turn.
Repeat 2nd row until 12 ins. have been worked, 1 ch. Turn.

Change to No. 1 hook
Work across long edge, making 83 sc. evenly, 3 ch. Turn.

1st row of pattern
1 dc. into 2nd sc., * 1 ch. 1 dc. into same place as last dc. 1 ch., y.o.h., insert hook into same place again as last 2 dc. and pull up a loop. Y.o.h. and draw through 2 loops, leaving 2 loops on hook. Skip 2 sc., 1 dc. into next sc., drawing through 2 loops and then drawing through the remaining 3 loops on hook. **Repeat** from * to end of row., 3 ch. Turn (27 grps.).

2nd row
1 dc. into center dc. of 1st grp., * 1 ch., 1 dc. into same place as last dc., 1 ch., y.o.h., insert hook into same place again as last 2 dc. and pull up a loop. Y.o.h. and draw through 2 loops, leaving 2 loops on hook, 1 dc. into center dc. of next grp., drawing through 2 loops and then drawing through the remaining 3 loops on hook. **Repeat** from * ending with, leave 2 loops on hook in last grp., 1 dc. into turning ch., drawing through 2 loops on hook and then drawing through the remaining 3 loops on hook. 3 ch. Turn. (The 2nd row forms the pattern.)
Repeat this row until work measures 21 ins. or length required to leg shaping.

Shaping the leg

1st row

* Pattern into 1st grp., leaving 2 loops on hook. 1 sc. into center dc. of next grp. and leaving 2 loops on hook., pattern in next grp. (1 grp. dec.).

Work in pattern across to last 2 grps. and with 2 loops on hook, work 1 sc. into center dc. of next grp., pattern into last grp., 3 ch. Turn. (1 grp. dec. at each end of row).

Work 3 rows straight in pattern and **repeat** from * 3 times more (19 grps. remain).

Work straight until work measures 26½ inches. (Adjust length here.) Fasten-off.

Turn work, skip 4 grps., and rejoin yarn. Work in pattern to last 4 grps., turn. Continue in pattern on these 11 grps., for instep, for 6 inches. Adjust length of foot (toe adds 2 inches). 1 ch. Turn.

Change to No. 2 hook

Work 36 sc. evenly across row, 1 ch. Turn. Continue in rows of sc., dec. 1 sc. at each end of next and every alternate row until 26 sc. remain. Then at each end of every row until 10 sc. remain. Fasten-off.

Join back seam of stocking with sc., or sew with a flat seam. Press seam lightly. With right side facing, rejoin yarn at back for heel. Work 32 sc. evenly across the 8 grps. left at back., 1 ch. Turn. Continue with rows of sc. turning each row with 1 ch. for 15 rows more.

Next row

1 sc. into each of the 1st 20 sc., dec. 1 sc. in next 2 sts. Turn.

Next row

1 sc. into each of the 1st 9 sc., dec. 1 sc. in next 2 sts. Turn.

Next row

1 sc. into each of the next 9 sc., dec. 1 sc. in next 2 sts. Turn.
Repeat the last row until all sts. have been worked (10 sc. remain).

Next row

With right side facing, 1 sc. into each of 10 sc., 1 sc. into each row end down side of heel, turn. (16 sts. at side of heel.)

Next row

1 sc. into each of the next 26 sc., 1 sc. into each row end down other side of heel. (42 sc. across row.) 1 ch. Turn.

Continue with rows of sc., dec. 1 sc. at each end of next and every alternate row until 32 sc. remain.

Continue straight until work measures the same as instep to beginning of toe shaping.

Shaping the toe

Dec. at each end of next and every alternate row until 18 sc. remain, then at each end of every row until 10 sc. remain. Fasten-off.

Making-up

Press lightly on wrong side of work under a damp cloth. Join foot seams and press lightly.

SUGGESTED COLORS
White
Bottle Green
Royal Blue
Chestnut Brown
Oxford
Grape

How to make a Tailored Suit with Raglan sleeves

Materials

WINTUK * Sport Yarn, 2 ply (2 oz. skeins), 20 (22, 24) ounces, steel hook No. 1; 1 inch wide elastic for waist; 5 button molds.

* Red Heart

Measurements (In Inches)

SKIRT

Length	26	27	28
Waist	24	26	28
Hips	36	38	40
Actual hip measurement of garment	38	40	42

JACKET

Bust	34	36	38
Actual bust measurement of finished garment	36	38	40
Length from back of neck	21	21	22
Sleeve	14	14	15

Gauge　　　　　2 groups to 1 inch in width and 3 rows to 1 inch

Actual st. for Tailored Suit

Method

SKIRT

Back and Front: the same. Make 120 (126 : 132) ch., loosely.

1st row
1 dc. into 6th ch. from hook, * 1 ch., 1 dc., into same ch. as last dc.
1 ch., y.o.h. insert hook into same ch. again as last 2 dc. and pull up a
loop. Y.o.h. and draw through 2 loops, leaving 2 loops on hook. Skip
2 ch. 1 dc. into next ch., drawing through 2 loops and then drawing
through remaining 3 loops on hook. **Repeat** from * to end of row
38 (40 : 42) grps. Turn with 3 ch.

2nd row
1 dc. into center dc., in 1st grp. * 1 ch., 1 dc. into same st, as last dc ,
1 ch., y.o.h. insert hook into same st,, again as last 2 dc. Pull up a loop,
y.o.h, and draw through 2 loops, leaving 2 loops on hook, 1 dc., into
center dc. of next grp., drawing through 2 loops and then drawing
through the remaining 3 loops on hook. **Repeat** from * ending,
leaving 2 loops on hook in last grp. 1 dc. into turning ch. Drawing
through 2 loops and then drawing through the remaining 3 loops on
hook. (This 2nd row forms the pattern.) Turn with 3 ch. **Repeat** this
until work measures 20 (21, 21) inches or length required to the dart
shaping.

Darts

Work 6 grps. in pattern, leaving 2 loops on hook, from last dc. of 6th
grp. * y.o.h., insert hook into center dc. of next grp. and pull up a
loop, y.o.h. Then pull through 3 loops, leaving 2 loops on hook, 1 dc.
into center dc. of next grp. * (1 grp. dec.) Continue in pattern until 8
grps. remain, leaving 2 loops on hook, **repeat** from * to *. Pattern to
end, work 3 rows straight, **repeat** the last 4 rows, 3 times more then
work straight until work measures 6 (6,7) ins. from beginning of dart
shaping. Fasten-off.

JACKET

Back

Make 114 (120 : 126) ch. loosely. Work straight in pattern 36 (38 : 40) grps. until work measures 11 ins. in length or length required to the raglan shaping. Mark each side with colored yarn before commencing raglan.

1st row
Work 1 grp. and then leaving 2 loops on hook, dec. in 2nd grp. as in darts in skirt. Work to last 3 grps., with 2 loops on hook, dec. in next grp., work to end.

2nd row
Work straight.

3rd row
Dec. as in 1st row.

4th row
Work straight.

5th row
Work straight.
Repeat these 5 rows, 5 times more.

Next row
Dec. row [31 rows in raglan for sizes 34 (36)]. Fasten-off. [10 (12 grps.) left for back of neck]; for size 38 continue thus:

32nd row
Work straight.

33rd row
Dec. row.

34th row
Work straight. Fasten-off.
(34 rows in raglan, 12 grps. left for back of neck.)

Pockets

Make 2, make 36 ch. loosely, (10 grps.). Work in pattern straight for 12 rows. Fasten-off.

Left Front

Make 66 (69 : 72) ch. loosely 20 (21 : 22) grps.
Work straight for 16 rows, insert pocket: beginning at side seam of left front, work 4 grps. in pattern. Pick up pocket and work along 10 grps., skip 10 grps. on main piece of front. Work along remaining grps. to end. Continue to work straight until you have as many rows as on the back, up to the raglan shaping. Mark beginning of raglan with colored yarn at side edge.

1st row Raglan
Work 1 grp. dec. in 2nd grp. as for Back, then work in pattern across.

2nd row
Work straight.

3rd row
Dec. row at raglan edge only.

4th and 5th rows
Work straight.
Repeat these 5 rows 2 times more.

16th row
Dec. row.

17th row

Work straight.
Repeat these 2 rows (16th and 17th) 7 times more for sizes 34 (36). Fasten-off [31 rows in raglan, 6 (7) grps. left for lapel]. For size 38— **Repeat** the 16th and 17th rows 8 times.

34th row

Work straight. Fasten-off (34 rows in raglan, 7 grps. left for lapel.) Mark left front for buttons.

Right Front

Work as for left front, reversing shaping of raglan and position of pockets. Make 5 evenly spaced buttonholes (marked on left front) the first 3 ins. from lower edge and the last one about 6 ins. down from the finish of the front.

To make a buttonhole

Method
Beginning at side edge, work across in pattern to the last grp. Work 2 of the 3 dc. grp. into the center dc. of last grp., 5 ch. Turn. Skip 1 grp. and sl. st. into the center dc. of the next grp., turn and work 5 sc. over the 5 ch. and sl. st. into the top of the dc. in the last grp. on previous row, 1 ch., 1 dc. into the same place as last dc. to complete the grp., leaving 2 loops on hook, 1 dc. into turning ch. 3 ch. Turn.

Next row
1 grp. into center dc. of 1st grp., skip 2 sc., 1 grp. into the next sc. Pattern to end.

Sleeves

Make 54 ch. (for sizes 34 and 36) 60 ch. for size (38) loosely 16 (18) grps. Work in pattern straight for 2 ins.

Next row

1 grp. into center dc. of 1st grp., leaving 2 loops on hook, work 1 dc., 1 ch., 1 dc., between the 1st and 2nd grps. Pattern to last grp. Having 2 loops on hook, work 1 dc., 1 ch., 1 dc., between the grp. just worked and the last grp. 1 dc., into turning ch.

Next row

In pattern, working 1 grp. into the 2 dc. at the beginning and end of row. 2 grps. inc. Work 5 rows plain. **Repeat** last 7 rows, 4 times more 26 (28) grps. Work straight until work measures 14 ins. or length required. Mark each end with colored yarn.

Raglan for sizes 34 (36)

1st row
Dec. 1 grp. each side as for Back.

2nd and 3rd row
Work straight.

4th row
Dec. each side.
Repeat last 3 rows, 9 times. Fasten-off.
(31 rows in raglan, 4 grps. left.)

For size 38

1st row
Dec. 1 grp. each side as for Back.

2nd row
Work straight.

3rd row
Work straight.

4th row
Dec. 1 grp. each side.
Repeat last 3 rows, 10 times. (34 rows in raglan, 4 grps. left.)

Making-up

Press each piece separately.

Skirt

Join side seams as near the edge as possible with a fine back st. Press seams.

Skirt Waist

Insert elastic as given in directions on page 12.

Jacket

Join sleeve raglans to back and front raglans. Press seams. Join underarm and sleeve seams and press. Sew back of pockets to fronts.

Collar

1st row
With Right side of work facing, attach yarn to Back Shou.der seam and work in pattern across Back of Neck, sl. st. over 2 grps. of Left sleeve. Turn.

2nd row
Work 12 (14, 14) grps. to Right sleeve, 2 grps. on sleeve, sl. st. over 2 grps. Turn.

3rd row
Work 16 (18, 18) grps., 2 grps. on Left sleeve, sl. st. over 2 grps. Turn.

4th row
Work 20 (22, 22) grps., 2 grps. on Right Front, sl. st. over 2 grps. Turn.

5th row
Work 24 (26, 26) grps., 2 grps. on Left Front, turn, leaving 3 grps. on each Front for lapel. Work straight in pattern over 26 (28, 28) grps. for 6 rows. Fasten-off.

BORDERS

Skirt

1st row
With Right side of work facing, attach yarn to side seams at lower edge and work sc. into side seam * 3 sc. into f. ch. in which 3 dc. have been worked. **Repeat** from * all around lower edge, working 1 sc. into side seam. Turn.

2nd row
1 sl. st. into each sc. taking great care not to work too tightly. Fasten-off.

Jacket

1st row
With Right side facing, attach yarn to Left Front at lower part of lapel and work 2 sc. into each row end to lower edge, 3 sc. into corner, 3 sc. into each f.ch. in which 3 dc. have been worked along lower edge, 3 sc. into corner and 2 sc. into each row end of Right Front up to lower part of lapel. Turn.

2nd row

Work 1 sl. st. into each sc. to Left Front lapel. Fasten-off. With wrong side of the work facing, attach yarn to lower part of lapel on Left Front and work sc. along lapels and collar with 3 sc. into each corner st. at lapel and collar. Turn.

3rd row

Work 1 sl. st. into each sc. Fasten-off. Work border on lower edge of sleeves and top of pockets.

Making-up

Give a final press. Sew on buttons—either bone or crochet buttons.

Crochet buttons

Method

Make 3 ch. and work 12 dc. into 3rd ch. from hook and without joining, work in rounds of sc. Inc. a sufficient number of times to keep work flat. Insert button mold and work rounds of sc. as necessary to fit mold. Break-off yarn, leaving sufficient to thread into a darning needle to weave through the last row of sc. and draw up to fit mold and fasten-off.

SUGGESTED COLORS
Blue Stone
Camel
Black
Antique Gold
Light Oxford
Bottle Green

How to make a Three-quarter length Coat with Raglan sleeves

Materials

Red Heart Sock & Sweater Yarn, 3 ply (2 oz. skeins), **40 (44) ounces**; steel hooks No. 1/0 (zero) and No. 2; 3 yds. lining, 3 button molds 1 inch in diameter.

Measurements

Bust
34—36 (38-40)

Length
Adjustable.

From back of neck
33 (34) ins.

**Lower edge to
  raglan armholes**
22 ins.

Raglan
11—(12)-ins.

Lower edge to pockets
15 ins.

Pocket
5½ ins. in width by 6 ins. in depth.

Width of back to armhole
20—(21)-ins. 10—(10½)-ins. each half.

**Width of each
  front to armhole**
14½ ins. (15)-ins.

Gauge (double yarn)
5 sts. to 1 inch, 7 rows to 2 ins.

View of enlarged st. of Three-quarter length Coat.

56

Method

Back

Left side—working with double yarn throughout, commence with 52 (58) ch.

1st row
1 dc. into 4th ch. from hook. 1 dc. into each ch. to end of row, 1 ch. Turn. 50 (56) sts.

2nd row
1 sc. into each dc., sc. in turning 3 ch. 3 ch. Turn. 50 (56) sc.

3rd row
Skip the 1st st., 1 dc. into each sc. to end of row, 1 ch. Turn.

4th row
1 sc. into each dc., ending with 1 sc. into turning ch., 3 ch. Turn.
Repeat the last 2 rows, 37 times or to length required ending with sc. row.

Shaping the raglan

Begin at Center Back.

1st row
Dc. to last 3 sts., dec. 1 dc., 1 dc. into last st., 1 ch. Turn.

2nd row
Sc. to end of row, 3 ch. Turn.

3rd row
Dc. to last 3 sts., dec. 1 dc., 1 dc. into last st., 1 ch. Turn.
Repeat the last 2 rows, 2 times (3 times).
Dec. at raglan side 1 st. on each row for 31 (33) rows. Fasten-off 15 (18) sc. remain at Back of Neck.

Back

Right side—work to correspond with Left side, reversing shapings.

Pockets

Make 2. Commence with 30 ch. Work in pattern (1 row dc. and 1 row sc.) on 28 sts. until work measures 6 ins. ending with sc. row. Fasten-off.

Front

Left side—Commence with 74 (80) ch.

1st row
1 dc. into 4th ch. from hook. 1 dc. into each ch. to end of row 72 (78) sts., 1 ch. Turn.

2nd row
1 sc. into each dc. to end, 3 ch. Turn.

3rd row
Skip 1st sc., 1 dc. into each sc. to end, 1 ch. Turn.

4th row
1 sc. into each dc., 1 sc. into turning ch., 3 ch. Turn.
Repeat the last 2 rows until 52 rows (26 ridges) have been worked or desired length to pocket is reached, ending with sc. row.
Insert pocket beginning at side seam, work 13 dc. pick up pocket, work 28 sts. across, skip 28 sts. on main part of work and continue in pattern along Front to end of row.
Work straight to correspond with Back to raglan.

Shaping the raglan

Work as for Back Raglan for 7 (9) rows. Continue dec. 1 st. on each row for raglan shaping and at the same time make Front dart.

Front dart

Next row

28(31) sc., dec. 1 sc. work to end.

Repeat this row on each alternate row (sc. row) until 9 (10) dec. for dart have been made and then dec. in the same st. every row for 7 rows.

Work another 7 rows with raglan shaping only. Fasten-off. 21 (23) sts. left on Front.

Mark Front edge for buttons.

Front

Right side—Work to correspond with Left Front, making buttonholes, inserting pockets and working raglan shaping at opposite side.

Buttonholes

Work on sc. row thus: 3 sc., 7 ch., skip 7 dc., sc to end of row, 3 ch. Turn.

Next row

Dc. to buttonhole, 1 dc. into each of 7 ch., dc. to end of row, 1 ch. Turn.

The 1st buttonhole is approx. 10½ ins. from lower edge and there are 7 ins. between buttonholes.

Sleeves

Commence with 70 (75) ch. Work in pattern (1 row dc., 1 row sc.) on 68 (73) sts. for 9 rows.

At each end of next row and every following 10th row inc. 1 sc. until work measures 15 ins. 78 (83) sts. ending with sc. row.

Shaping raglan

1st row

1 dc., dec. 1 dc., work to last 3 dc., dec. 1 dc., 1 dc., 1 ch. Turn.

2nd row

1 sc., dec. 1 st. 34 (36) sc. Dec. 1 st. (Mark this st. with colored cotton) 34 (37) sc., dec. 1 st., 1 sc., 3 ch. Turn.

3rd row

Work straight across, 1 ch., turn.

4th row

1 sc., dec. 1 st. Work to last 3 sts., dec. 1 st., 1 sc. Turn.

5th row

Work straight across, 1 ch. Turn.

6th row

1 sc., dec. 1 st., sc. to center of sleeve, dec. 1 st. to correspond with st. marked with colored cotton. (Mark this st. at each center dec.) sc. to last 3 dc. dec. 1 st., 1 sc., 3 ch. Turn.

Repeat the last 4 rows, 4 (5) times. (48 sts. each size.)
Continue dec. at the center of sleeve on every 4th row and at the same time dec. at each end of the following 16 rows of raglan. Fasten-off. (12 sts. remain at top of sleeve.)

Making-up

Press each piece separately. Lay pieces on lining and cut round allowing 1 inch for turnings. Sew in sleeves or crochet together with a dc. Press seams. Sew or crochet center back, side and sleeve seams and press. Sew Back of pockets to coat.

Collar

1st row

With Right side of coat facing, attach yarn (double) to Back seam of raglan on Right Front. Work 30 (36) sc. along Back of Neck and 6 (8) sc. along top of sleeve, sl. st. over 3 sts. Turn.

2nd row

Sc. into 48 (55) sts., sl. st. over 3 sts. along top of sleeve. Turn.

3rd row

Sc. into 54 (61) sts., sl. st. along 3 sts. Turn.

4th row

Sc. into 60 (67) sts., sl. st. along 3 sts. Turn.

5th row

Sc. into 66 (73) sts., sl. st. along 3 sts. Turn.

6th row

Sc. into 72 (79) sts., sl. st. along 3 sts. Turn.

7th row

Sc. into 78 (85) sts., sl. st. along 3 sts., 2 ch. Turn.

8th row

Sc. into 84 (94) sts., 2 ch. Turn, leaving 6 sts. on each front for lapel. Work straight on 84 (94) sc. for 22 rows, turning at each end with 2 ch. Fasten-off.

Borders

With right side of work facing, join yarn to Left Front at the lower part of lapel and work 1 sc. into end of sc. row. Then 2 sc. into dc. row end to lower edge of coat, 3 sc. into corner, 1 sc. into each st. along lower edge, 3 sc. into corner and 2 sc. into dc. row ends. 1 sc. into sc. row ends to lower part of lapel on Right Front. Turn 1 sl. st. into each sc. all around, taking care not to work too tightly. Fasten-off.

Rejoin yarn to Left Front edge with wrong side of work facing and work border along edges of lapels and collar, working 3 sc. into corner of lapel and collar.

Work same border on cuffs and pockets.

Making-up

Give coat a final press and sew on buttons, either bone or crochet, and insert lining.

Crochet buttons

Method

Button molds, using yarn singly and No. 2 hook make 3 ch. work 12 tr. into 3rd ch. from hook, then work in rounds of sc., inc. a sufficient number of times to keep work flat. Insert button mold and work rounds of sc. as necessary to fit mold. Cut yarn, leaving a long enough end to thread into a darning needle and weave into last row of sc. and pull up to mold.

SUGGESTED COLORS
Oxford
Black
Camel
Florentine Blue
Bottle Green
Sunset Red

How to make a
Car Coat

Materials

WINTUK * Sport Yarn, 2 ply (2 oz. skeins): 16 (18) ounces; steel hook No. 1/0 (zero); 6 or 7 button molds.

* Red Heart

Measurements
34—36, (38—40) in. bust; length adjustable.

Gauge
3 grps. to 1 inch, 4 rows to 1 inch.

Actual st. for Car Coat

Method

Pattern throughout.

1st row
1 sc. and 1 dc. into 2nd ch. from hook, * skip 1 ch., 1 sc. and 1 dc. into next ch. **Repeat** from * to end of row, 1 ch. Turn.

2nd row
1 sc. and 1 dc. into 1st dc. * Skip 1 sc., 1 sc. and 1 dc. into next dc. **Repeat** from * to end of row, 1 ch. Turn.
Repeat 2nd row for pattern.

Back

Commence with 108 (120) ch. 54 (60) grps. Work 15 ins. in pattern or until desired length to Armhole is reached.

Shaping the Armholes

1st row
Beginning at Right Armhole, sl. st. over 3 grps. 1 ch. Work to last 3 grps. Sl. st. into next st, 1 ch. 48 (54) grps. Turn.

2nd row
Work straight row without dec. Turn.

3rd row
1 ch., 1 sc. into 1st dc., skip 1 sc. and work 1 sc. and 1 dc. into next dc. Work to last grp., 1 sc. into last sc. Turn.

4th row

1 ch., skip 1 sc., 1 sc. and 1 dc. into next dc. Work to last grp. sl. st. into last sc. Turn.

Repeat 3rd and 4th rows, 2 times (3 times) more, 42 (46) grps. Work straight until work measures 8—(8½) ins. above underarm. Turn.

Shaping the Shoulders

Beginning at Right Shoulder, sl. st. over 4 grps. 1 ch., 1 sc. and 1 dc. into next dc. Work to last 4 grps., sl. st. into next st. Turn.

Repeat this row 2 times. Fasten-off. [18 (22) grps. remain at Back of Neck.]

Pockets

Make 2. Commence with 30 ch. Work in pattern on 15 grps. for 6 ins. Fasten-off.

Left Front

Commence with 60 (66) ch. Work as for Back. 30 (33) grps., until work measures 8½ ins.

Insert pockets 2 ins. (6 grps.) from side edge of Front, work 15 grps. on pocket, skip 15 grps. on Front and continue in pattern to end of row. Turn. Work straight to Armhole as for Back.

Shaping the Armhole

Work as for Right Armhole of Back, then straight until work measures 6—(6½) ins. from underarm 24 (26) grps.

Shaping the Neck

1st row

Beginning at Front edge, sl. st. over 6 grps., work to end of row. Turn.

2nd row

Work to last grp., sl. st. into next st. Turn.

3rd row

1 ch., sc. in 1st dc., skip sc. and work 1 sc. and 1 dc. into next dc., work to end of row. Turn.

Repeat 2nd and 3rd rows, 2 (3) times more.

Work straight until armhole measures the same as Back.

Shaping the Shoulder

Work as for Right Shoulder of Back. Fasten-off. Mark position on Front edge for buttons (6 or 7 as desired) having 1 button in 3rd row below Neck edge and the others about 3—(3½) ins. apart.

Right Front

Work to correspond with Left Front, reversing all shapings and working buttonholes opposite each marker for the buttons on Left Front, thus:

1st buttonhole row—Front edge

1 sc. and 1 dc. into 1st dc., 1 sc. into next dc., 5 ch., skip 2 grps., 1 sc. and 1 dc. into next dc. Continue in pattern to end of row. Turn.

2nd buttonhole row

Work in pattern to buttonhole, 1 sc. and 1 dc. into 2nd ch., skip 1 ch., 1 sc. and 1 dc. into next ch. Skip 1 ch., 1 sc. and 1 dc. into next sc., 1 sc. and 1 dc. into next dc. Turn.

Sleeves

Commence with 62 (68) ch., work in pattern for 3 ins., 31 (34) grps. Inc. in next 2 rows thus:

1st row

1 ch., 2 sc. and 1 dc. into 1st dc. Work to last grp., 1 sc. and 1 dc. into next dc., 1 sc. into last sc. Turn.

2nd row

1 ch., 1 sc. and 1 dc. into 1st sc., 1 sc. and 1 dc. into next dc. Work across, ending with 1 sc. and 1 dc. in last sc. (1 grp. inc. at each end of row.)

Repeat these 2 rows every 3 ins. (from last inc.), 4 times more 41 (44) grps. Work straight until desired length to underarm is reached.

Sleeve Cap

1st row

Sl. st. over 3 grps., work to last 3 grps. Turn.

Then dec. 1 st. at each end of the row as for armhole of Back on the next 20 (22) rows.

Next row

Sl. st. over 2 grps. work to last 2 grps. Turn.

Repeat last row, once. Fasten-off [7 (8) grps. remain at top of sleeve.]

Collar

Commence with 88 (92) ch. Work in pattern on 44 (46) grps. for 4 ins.

1st dec. row

Sl. st. over 3 (4) grps., 1 ch., 1 sc. and 1 dc. into next dc. Work across to last 3 (4) grps. Sl. st. into next st. Turn.

2nd row

Sl. st. over 5 grps., 1 ch., 1 sc., and 1 dc. into next dc. Work across to last 5 grps., sl. st. into next st. Turn.

Repeat 2nd row once more. Fasten-off [18 (22) grps. remain at Back of Neck.]

Making-up

Press all pieces separately with a damp cloth, a hot iron and a light hand. Join Shoulder seams and press. Sew in Sleeves, press and join side and sleeve seams. Press. Sew on Collar and Back of Pockets.

Crochet Buttons

Method

Make 3 ch., work 12 dc. into 3rd ch. from hook and without joining, work in rounds of sc., inc. a sufficient number of times to keep work flat. Insert button mold and work rounds of sc. as necessary to fit mold.

SUGGESTED COLORS
Sunset Red
Grape
Bottle Green
Florentine Blue
Camel
Oxford

How to make a
Two-colored Dress

Materials

Red Heart Super Fingering, 3 Ply (1 oz. skeins): 11 (12, 13) ounces of Natural—main color and 5 (6, 7) ounces of Wood Brown; crochet hook size E and steel hooks No. 1/0 (zero) and No. 2/0 (double zero).

Measurements
To fit 34—(36 : 38)-ins. bust; length from shoulder—38-(41 : 43) ins. (adjustable.)

Gauge with Size E Hook
2 groups = 1¾ inches;
5 pattern rows = 2½ inches.

View of enlarged st. of Two-colored Dress.

Method

Front and Back (alike.) Commence with Size E hook in main color and 104 (112 : 120) ch.

1st row
Leaving the last loop of each on hook, work 2 dc. into 4th ch. from hook, y.o.h. and draw through 3 loops on hook (hlf. grp.), 3 ch. leaving the last loop of each on hook. 3 dc. into same ch., y.o.h. and draw through 4 loops on hook (hlf grp.) * Skip 3 ch., leaving the last loop of each on hook, 3 dc. into next ch., y.o.h. and draw through 4 loops on hook. 3 ch. leaving the last loop of each on hook, 3 dc. into same ch., y.o.h. and draw through all loops on hook (these 3 dc., 3 ch. and 3 dc. form 1 grp). **Repeat** from * to end, turn 26 (28 : 30) grps.

2nd row
3 ch. (this forms 1st dc. of a hlf. grp.) 2 dc. into top of 1st hlf. grp. * skip 3 ch. (hlf. grp., 3 ch., hlf. grp.) into top of next hlf. grp. This gives a complete grp. between the grp. of last row. **Repeat** from * ending with skip 3 ch. 1 hlf. grp. into top of last hlf. grp. Turn.

3rd row
3 ch., 1 grp. into top of 1st hlf. grp. * Skip 3 ch., 1 grp. into top of next hlf. grp. **Repeat** from * ending with skip 3 ch., 1 grp. into top of last hlf. grp.

4th row
As 2nd row. End thus: Leave loop of last grp. on a safety pin, join contrast yarn to top of 1st hlf. grp. at opposite end of work.

5th row-right side
With contrast yarn make 2 ch. * 1 sc. in top of next hlf. grp., 3 sc. into the 3 ch. sp.; skip next hlf. grp. **Repeat** from * ending with 1 sc. in top of last hlf. grp. Pick up loop from safety pin and draw through loop on hook. Break-off contrast yarn—101 (109 : 117) sc. Turn.

6th row

Main color, 3 ch. 1 grp. worked over 1 sc. into grp. of previous row. * Skip 3 sc. 1 grp., over next sc. into grp. of previous row. **Repeat** from * ending with 1 grp. over 1 sc. into last grp. of previous row.

(Rows 2—6 inclusive form the pattern.) Continue straight for 12 (14 : 16) ins. (If a longer garment is required extra length should be added on here.)

Now

Change to No. 2/0 hook and continue in pattern until work measures 19—(21 : 23) ins. from beginning.

Then

Change to No. 1/0 hook and continue in pattern until work measures 31½—(34 : 36) ins. from beginning, ending at the end of the 6th row of pattern.

Shaping the Armholes

Main color, omit 1st hlf. grp. inside the 1st and last hlf. grp. at each end of the next 4 grp. rows, 22 (24, 26) grps. Continue straight until work measures 6½—(7 : 7) ins. from beginning of shaping, ending with 4th row of pattern. Fasten-off.

Shaping neck and Shoulders

With right side facing and using contrast yarn, * 1 sc. into top of 1st hlf. grp. 3 sc. in the 3 ch. sp. **Repeat** from * 7—(8 : 9) times, ending with 1 sc. into top of next hlf. grp. Turn.

Next row

Main color, join yarn into hlf. grp. into which 1 sc. has been worked, hlf. grp. over same hlf. grp. * 1 grp. over next. 1 sc., **repeat** from * ending with 1 hlf. grp. over last sc. Turn. 7½(8½—9½) grps. Turn.

Next row

Sl. st. over 1½ grps. (2 grps. : 2½ grps.) pattern into 4½ grps. (5 grps. : 5½ grps.) Sl. st. into next st. Turn.

Next row

Sl. st. over 1½ grps. (1½ grps. : 1½ grps.) pattern into 2 (3 : 3) grps. Sl. st. into next st. Turn.

Next row

Sl. st. over 0 (1 : 1) grp., pattern hlf. grp. into top of next hlf. grp. 1 grp. into top of next hlf. grp. and hlf. grp. into top of last hlf. grp. Fasten-off.

Left Shoulder

Skip 6 grps. at neck edge and join in contrast yarn. Work Neck and Shoulder shapings to correspond with Right Shoulder. Fasten-off.

Making-up

Press each piece over a dry cloth or skim over (not touching garment) with a steam iron.

Neck Back

Work 72 sc. across Neck shaping for 8 rows with contrast yarn.

9th row

Dec. 5 st. evenly placed. Fasten-off.

Neck Front

Work as for Back.

Making-up

Match patterns, join Side and Shoulder seams.

Method No. 1
Sew with fine back stitch as near the edge as possible.

Method No. 2
Crochet seams together thus: Side seams—2 sc. into each grp. row end and 1 sc. into each sc. row end. Shoulder seam—1 sc. into each st.

Making-up

Sew borders at Neck with a flat seam.

Armhole borders

Work 82 sc. round Armholes for 6 rows, dec. on alternate rows, 1 sc. each side of Shoulder seam.

Lower edge of dress

Work 3 rows sc., 3 sc. over 3 ch. sp., 1 sc. between grps. Finish off with a crochet cord for a belt.

Method
Make 6 ch. and join with a sl. st., work 1 sc. in each st. Without joining rows and working into back loop of st. **only**, continue working in sc. until cord is desired length. Make 2 bobbles or pompons and attach one to each end of cord.

SUGGESTED ALTERNATE COLORS

Skipper Blue and Blue Jewel
Wine and Pearl Grey
Black and White
Meadow Green and Scarlet

How to make a Classic Teenager's Dress

Materials

Directions are given for Size 10. Changes for Sizes 12, 14 and 16 are in parentheses.

WINTUK* Sport Yarn, 2 Ply (2 oz. skeins) = 16 (18 : 20 : 22) ounces, crochet Hook, size G.

*Red Heart

Measurements

Size 32½ (34 : 36 : 38) - ins. bust. Length from underarm to lower edge, excluding border, 33 (34 : 35 : 36)-ins.

Gauge:

3 shells to 2 ins.; 2 rows to 1 inch.

Edging

Actual st. for Classic Teenager's Dress

Method

DRESS

Dress is worked in one piece from lower edge to underarm. Starting at lower edge, ch. 170 (182 : 194 : 206), having 9 ch. to 2 inches, to measure 38 (40 : 43 : 46) inches.

1st row
Sc. in 2nd ch. from hook, * ch. 2, skip next 2 ch., sc. in next ch. **Repeat from * across**—56 (60 : 64 : 68) ch.-2 sps. Ch. 3, turn.

2nd row
* In next ch.-2 sp. make 3 dc.—**shell in sp. made**. Repeat from * across ending with dc. in last sc.—56 (60 : 64 : 68) shells. Ch. 3, turn.

3rd row
Skip first dc., 3 dc. in next sc.—**shell over shell made; * skip next 2 dc.,** 3 dc. in next dc.—**another shell over shell made**. Repeat from * across, ending with skip next 2 dc., dc. in top of turning chain. Ch. 3, turn. Repeat 3rd row for pattern. Work in pattern until total length is 18 (18½ : 19 : 19) inches. Ch. 3, turn.

Next row
Shell over each of next 14 (15 : 16 : 17) shells—Front; place a contrasting colored strand (marker) in work between last shell used and following shell; shell over each of next 28 (30 : 32 : 34) shells—Back; place another marker in work as before; shell over each remaining shell for other Front; dc. in top of turning chain. Ch. 3, turn.

NOTE: Carry markers up on each row between the 2 shells directly above. Now work decrease rows as follows:

1st Dec. row

* Shell over each shell to within one shell before next marker, (skip next 2 dc., 2 dc. in next dc.—**2-dc. shell made**) twice. Repeat from * once more; shell over each remaining shell, dc. in top of turning chain. Ch. 3, turn.

2nd Dec. row

* Shell over each shell to within one shell before next 2-dc. shell, skip 2 dc., 2 dc. in next dc., skip next 2 dc., (dc. in next dc., skip next dc.) twice; 2 dc. in next dc. Repeat from * once more; shell over each remaining shell, dc. in top of turning chain. Ch. 3, turn.

3rd Dec. row

Skip first dc., 3 dc. in next dc., * skip 2 dc., 3 dc., in next dc. Repeat from * across, dc. in top of turning chain—1 shell decreased on each side of each marker over last 3 rows—52 (56 : 60 : 64) shells. Ch. 3, turn. Work 2 rows even, then repeat the 3 decrease rows once more. Remove markers. Ch. 3, turn. Work even over 48 (52 : 56 : 60) shells until total length is 24 (25 : 25 : 26) inches.

Inc. row

Shell over each of next 3 (5 : 6 : 9) shells, (skip next dc., 3 dc. in next dc.) 3 times—**one shell increased;** * shell over each of next 6 (8 : 12 : 18) shells, (skip next dc., 3 dc. in next dc.) 3 times. Repeat from * 4 (3 : 2 : 1) times more; shell over each remaining shell, dc. in top of turning chain—54 (57 : 60 : 63) shells. Ch. 3, turn. Work even over these shells until total length is 32 (33 : 34 : 35) inches. Ch. 3, turn.

NOTE: One inch is allowed for stretching.

RIGHT FRONT

Shaping the Raglan

1st row

Shell over each of next 12 (13 : 14 : 15) shells, skip next dc., dc. in next dc. Do not work over remaining shells. Ch. 3, turn.

2nd row

Skip first 4 dc., 3 dc. in next dc.—**one shell decreased at armhole edge**; shell over each of next 10 (11 : 12 : 13) shells, dc. in top of turning chain. Ch. 3, turn.

3rd row

Shell over each shell across, dc. in top of turning chain. Ch. 3, turn.

4th row

Dec. one shell at beg. of row, complete row as for 2nd row. Ch. 3, turn.

5th row

Repeat 3rd row—10 (11 : 12 : 13) shells. Ch. 3, turn. Mark end of last row to indicate beg. of neck edge. Now dec. one shell at beg. of **every** row, thus shaping both armhole and neck edges, until one shell remains. Break off and fasten.

BACK

Shaping the Raglan

Skip next 3 shells on last row before Right Front Raglan Shaping. Attach yarn before next shell, ch. 3 and work a shell over each of next 24 (25 : 26 : 27) shells. Do not work over remaining shells. Ch. 3, turn. Dec. one shell at beg. of **every** row until 11 shells remain. Break off and fasten.

LEFT FRONT

Shaping the Raglan

Skip next 3 shells on last row before Back Raglan Shaping. Attach yarn before next shell, ch. 3 and work to correspond with Right Front, reversing shapings.

SLEEVES

Starting at lower edge, ch. 32 (35 : 38 : 41) having 9 ch. to 2 inches. to measure 7 (7½ : 8 : 8½) inches. Work as for Dress until the 3rd row has been completed, having 10 (11 : 12 : 13) shells. Repeat 3rd row until total length is 3 (3 : 3½ : 4) inches. Ch. 3, turn.

Next row

3 dc. in first dc., (skip next dc., shell in next dc.) twice—**one shell increased at beg. of row**; shell over each shell to within last shell, (skip next dc., 3 dc. in next dc.) twice—**one shell increased at end of row**; skip next dc., dc. in top of turning chain. Ch. 3, turn. Work 3 inches even in pattern. Inc. one shell at both ends of next row and every 3 inches thereafter, 3 times in all—18 (19 : 20 : 21) shells. Work even until total length is 16½ (17 : 17 : 17½) inches. Break off and fasten. Turn.

Shaping the Raglan

1st row

Skip first 2 shells for underarm; attach yarn before next shell, ch. 3, work shell over 14 (15 : 16 : 17) shells. Do not work over remaining shells. Ch. 3, turn. Dec. one shell at beg. of next row and **every** row thereafter until one shell remains. Break off and fasten.
Block to measurements. Sew sleeve seams. Sew in sleeves.

EDGING

With right side facing, attach yarn to lower left front corner.

1st row
Working along opposite side of starting chain, * in next ch.-2 sp. make dc., 3 tr. and dc.—**large shell made**; sc. in next sp. Repeat from * along entire lower edge; working along ends of rows, continue to repeat from * along right front edge to shoulder; work along neck edge as follows: (skip 2 dc., large shell in next dc., skip 2 dc., sc. in next dc.) 5 times; skip 2 dc., large shell in next dc.; continue edging as before, along left front neck edge. Break off and fasten. Work Edging along each sleeve edge. Join with sl. st. to first sc. Break off and fasten. Leaving Edging to extend free, sew edge of left front to right front at base of edging.

CORD

Using 2 strands of yarn held together, make a chain 15 inches longer than desired waist measurement. Sc. in 2nd ch. from hook and in each ch. across. Break off and fasten. Draw cord through shells at desired waistline (below inc. row) and tie in a knot at front.

SUGGESTED COLORS

Cerise
Apple Green
Baby Aqua
Evening Violet

How to make a Coat and Dress

Materials

Knitting Worsted, 4 Ply

SIZES

	10	12	14	16	18
DRESS					
Ounces	20	22	24	26	28
COAT—¾ LENGTH					
Ounces	26	28	32	36	38
COAT—⅞ LENGTH					
Ounces	30	32	36	40	42

Crochet Hooks, Sizes F and H
Neck Opening Zipper, 20 inch length.
1 large hook and eye for Coat; 1 small hook and eye for Dress.

BLOCKING MEASUREMENTS

	Sizes				
	10	12	14	16	18
Body Bust Size (In Inches)					
	31	32	34	36	38
Hips	33	34	36	38	40

View of enlarged st. of Coat and Dress.

ACTUAL CROCHETING MEASUREMENTS

Dress

Bust	34	35	37	39	41
Hips	36	37	39	41	43
Length from back of neck to lower edge					
	38¼	39	40	40	41
Length from underarm to lower edge					
	31¼	31¾	32	32	32½
Length of sleeve seam					
	4	4	4½	4½	5
Width across sleeve at upper arm					
	12	12½	13	13½	14

Coat

Bust	39	40	42	44	46
Length from back of neck to lower edge					
¾ length	29	29½	30½	30½	31
⅞ length	33	33½	34½	34½	35
Length from underarm to lower edge					
¾ length	21	21	21	21	21
⅞ length	25	25	25	25	25
Width around lower edge					
	39	40	42	44	46
Length of sleeve seam					
	13	13½	14	14	14½
Width across sleeve at upper arm					
	14	14	15	15	16

Gauge

Size H hook—5 sc., and 4 ch.-1 sps., to 2 inches, 7 rows to 2 inches.

Method

DRESS

Starting at lower edge with Size H hook (having 9 ch. to 2 inches) make a ch. of 162 (166 : 176 : 184 : 194) stitches to measure 36 (37 : 39 : 41 : 43) inches. Being careful not to twist the ch., join with sl. st. to form a ring.

1st round (right side)
Ch. 1, sc. in joining, ch. 1, skip next ch., * sc. in next ch., ch. 1, skip next ch. Repeat from * around. Join with sl. st. to first sc. Ch. 1, turn. There are 81 (83 : 88 : 92 : 97) sc. on round.

2nd round
Sc. in joining, ch. 1, skip next ch. 1, * sc. in next sc., ch. 1, skip next ch.-1. Repeat from * around. Join as before. Ch. 1, turn. Repeat 2nd round for pattern. Work in pattern until total length is 19 (19 : 20 : 20 : 21) inches. Now work in rows as follows:

1st row
Sc. in joining ch. 1, * sc. in next sc., ch. 1. Repeat from * across, ending with sc. in last sc. Do not join. Ch. 1, turn.

2nd row
Sc. in first sc., * ch. 1, sc. in next sc. Repeat from * across Ch. 1, turn. Repeat 2nd row until total length is 22½ (22 : 23 : 23½ : 24½) inches. Change to Size F hook.

Next row
Sc. in first sc., * ch. 1, sc. in next sc. Repeat from * across. Ch. 1, next ch.-1, sc. in next sc.—**1 ch.-1 sp. decreased**; (ch. 1, sc. in next sc.) 40 (40 : 43 : 45 : 48) times, skip next ch. 1, sc. in next sc.—another sp. decreased; (ch. 1, sc. in next sc.) 19 (20 : 21 : 22 : 23) times—2 ch.-1 sps. decreased on row. Ch. 1, turn.

Following row
Sc. in first sc., ch. 1, (sc. in next sc., ch. 1) 18 (19 : 20 : 21 : 22) times. Draw up a loop in each of next 2 sc., yarn over and draw through all loops on hook—**1 sc. decreased**; ch. 1, (sc. in next sc., ch. 1) 39 (39 :

42 : 44 : 47) times, dec. 1 sc. over next 2 sc., (ch. 1, sc. in next sc.) 19 (20 : 21 : 22 : 23) times—2 sc. decreased on row. Ch. 1, turn. With contrasting colored thread, mark each decrease. Work 6 rows without decreasing. Dec. 1 ch.-1 sp. before first decrease and 1 ch-1 sp. after 2nd decrease on next row. Dec. 1 sc. over each decreased sp. on following row. There remain 77 (79 : 84 : 88 : 93) sc. on row. Remove markers. Work without decreasing until total length is 25½ (25½ : 26 : 26½ : 27½) inches. Change to Size H hook and work without decreasing until total length is 31¼ (31¾ : 32 : 32 : 32½) inches or desired length to underarm, ending with right side row. Ch. 1, turn.

Right Back Raglan Armhole Shaping

1st row
Sc. in first sc. (ch. 1, sc. in next sc.) 16 (17 : 18 : 19 : 20) times. Ch. 1, turn. Work over this section as follows:

2nd row
Sc. in first sc., skip next ch. 1, sc. in next sc. (1 ch -1 sp. decreased at armhole edge); * ch. 1, sc. in next sc. Repeat from * across. Ch. 1, turn.

3rd row
Sc. in first sc., ch. 1, * sc. in next sc., ch. 1. Repeat from * across to within last 2 sc., dec. 1 sc. over last 2 sc. Ch. 1, turn.

4th row
Work in pattern without decreasing. Ch. 1, turn.

Next row
Decreasing 1 ch.-1 sp. at armhole edge, work in pattern across. Ch. 1, turn.

Following row
Decreasing 1 sc. at armhole edge, work in pattern across. Ch. 1, turn.
Work in pattern without decreasing for 0 (1 : 1 : 1 : 1) row.

Next row

Decreasing 1 ch.-1 sp. at armhole edge, work in pattern across. Ch. 1, turn.

Following row

Decreasing 1 sc. at armhole edge, work in pattern across. Ch. 1, turn. Repeat last 2 rows until there are on row

Sc.	6	7	7	8	8

Break off and fasten.

Front Raglan Armhole Shaping

1st row

With wrong side facing, skip next 4 sc. on last long row worked before Back Armhole Shaping, attach yarn to next sc., ch. 1, sc. in same sc., (ch. 1, sc. in next sc.)

Times	34	34	37	39	42

Ch. 1, turn.

2nd row

Sc. in first sc., dec. first ch.-1 sp., ch. 1, * sc. in next sc., ch. 1. Repeat from * across to within last 2 sc., sc. in next sc., dec. last ch.-1 sp. Ch. 1, turn.

3rd row

Dec. 1 sc. over first 2 sc., ch. 1, * sc. in next sc., ch. 1. Repeat from * across, decreasing 1 sc. over last 2 sc. Ch. 1, turn.

4th row

Work in pattern without decreasing. Ch. 1, turn.

Next row

Decreasing 1 ch.-1 sp. at both ends of row, work in pattern across. Ch. 1, turn.

Following row

Decreasing 1 sc. at both ends of row, work in pattern across. Ch. 1, turn. Work in pattern without decreasing for 0 (1 : 1 : 1 : 1) row.

Next row

Decreasing 1 ch.-1 sp. at both ends of row, work in pattern across. Ch. 1, turn.

Following row

Decreasing 1 sc. at both ends of row, work in pattern across. Ch. 1, turn. Repeat last 2 rows until there remain 21 (21 : 22 : 26 : 27) sc. on row.

Neck Shaping

1st row

Sc. in first sc. dec. first ch.-1 sp., (ch. 1, sc. in next sc.) 4 (4 · 4 : 6 : 6) times, dec. last ch.-1 sp. Ch. 1, turn.

2nd row

Dec. 1 sc. over first 2 sc., * ch. 1, sc. in next sc. Repeat from * across, decreasing 1 sc. over last 2 sc. Ch. 1, turn.

3rd row

Decreasing 1 ch.-1 sp. at armhole edge and at neck edge, work in pattern across. Repeat last 2 rows until 3 sc. remain on row. Keeping neck edge even, continue to shape armhole edge as before until 1 sc. remains. Break off and fasten. Skip next 7 (7 : 8 : 8 : 9) sc. on last row before Neck Shaping, attach yarn to next sc., ch. 1, sc. in same sc., dec. next ch.-1., work in pattern across, decreasing 1 ch.-1 sp. at armhole edge. Ch. 1, turn. Continue to shape armhole and neck edges to correspond with opposite side, reversing shapings.

Left Back Raglan Armhole Shaping

1st row

With wrong side facing, skip next 4 sc. on last long row worked before Front Armhole Shaping, attach yarn to next sc., ch. 1, sc. in same sc., * ch. 1, sc. in next sc. Repeat from * across. Ch. 1, turn.

2nd row

Work in pattern across, decreasing 1 ch.-1 sp. at armhole edge. Ch. 1, turn. Continue to work to correspond with Right Back Armhole Shaping, reversing shapings.

Sleeves

Starting at lower edge with Size F hook (having 5 ch. to 1 inch), make a chain of 54 (56 : 60 : 62 : 64) stitches to measure 11 (11¼ : 12 : 12¼ : 12¾) inches.

1st row (right side)

Sc. in 2nd ch. from hook, * ch. 1, skip next ch., sc. in next ch. Repeat from * across. There are 27 (28 : 30 : 31 : 32) sc. on row. Ch. 1, turn.

2nd row

Sc. in first sc., * ch. 1, sc. in next sc. Repeat from * across. Ch. 1, turn. Repeat 2nd row 4 times more. Change to Size H hook and continue in pattern until length is

| inches | 4 | 4 | 4½ | 4½ | 5 |

Do not ch. 1 at end of last row. Turn.

Raglan Top Shaping

1st row

Sl. st. in first sc., (sl. st. in next ch. and following sc.) twice; ch. 1, sc. in same sc. where last sl. st. was made, (ch. 1, sc. in next sc.)

| Times | 22 | 23 | 25 | 26 | 27 |

Ch. 1, turn. Starting with 2nd row and omitting the Neck Shaping, shape top same as Front Raglan Armhole Shaping, until there remain on row

Sc.	3	2	2	3	2

Break off and fasten.

Block to measurements. Sew Sleeve seams. Sew in sleeves.

Neck Edging

1st row

With right side of work facing, using Size H hook and being careful to keep work flat, sc. evenly around neck edge. Ch. 1, turn.

2nd row

Sc. in each sc. around. Turn.

3rd row

Sl. st. in each sc. around; then, being careful to keep work flat, sc. closely along back opening edges.

Break off and fasten. Sew in zipper.

Sew small hook and eye to corners at neck.

COAT

Body

Starting at lower edge with Size H hook (having 9 ch. to 2 inches), make a chain of

Stitches	176	180	188	198	206
to measure					
Inches	39	40	42	44	46

1st row

Work as for first row of Sleeve of Dress. There are on row

Sc.	88	90	94	99	103

Ch. 1, turn.

2nd row
Repeat 2nd row of Sleeve. Repeat 2nd row until length is for ¾ length

Inches	21	21	21	21	21

For ⅞ length

Inches	25	25	25	2ɔ	25

ending with a wrong-side row. Ch. 1, turn.

Right Front Raglan Armhole Shaping

1st row
Sc. in first sc., (ch. 1, sc. in next sc.)

Times	19	20	21	23	24

Ch. 1, turn. Work over this section only.

2nd row
Work in pattern across. Ch. 1, turn.

3rd row
Sc. in first sc., (ch. 1, sc. in next sc.)

Times	18	19	20	22	23

dec. next ch.-1 sp. Ch. 1, turn.

4th row
Dec. 1 sc. over first 2 sc., * ch. 1, sc. in next sc. Repeat from * across.
Ch. 1, turn. Work without decreasing for

Rows	0	2	2	2	2

Next row
Work in pattern across, decreasing 1 ch.-1 sp. at armhole edge. Ch. 1, turn.

Following row
Work in pattern across, decreasing 1 sc. at armhole edge. Ch. 1, turn.
Repeat last 4 rows

Times	0	0	0	2	2

Next row
Work in pattern across, decreasing 1 ch.-1 sp. at armhole edge. Ch. 1,
turn.

Following row
Decreasing 1 sc. at armhole edge, work in pattern across. Ch. 1, turn.
Repeat last 2 rows until there remain 13 (14 : 14 : 18 : 18) sc. on row,
ending at armhole edge.

Next row
Work in pattern across, decreasing 1 ch.-1 sp. at armhole edge. Ch. 1,
turn.

Neck Shaping

1st row
Dec, 1 sc. over first 2 sc., (ch. 1, sc. in next sc.)
times   7   7   7   9   9
Ch. 1, turn.

2nd row
Decreasing 1 ch.-1 sp. at both ends of row, work in pattern across.
Ch. 1, turn.

3rd row
Decreasing 1 sc. at both ends of row, work in pattern across. Ch. 1,
turn. Repeat 2nd and 3rd rows alternately until 4 sc. remain on row.
Keeping neck edge straight, continue to shape armhole edge as before
until 1 sc. remains. Break off and fasten.

Back Raglan Armhole Shapings

1st row

With right side facing, skip next 4 sc. on last long row worked before armhole shaping, attach yarn to next sc., ch. 1, sc. in same sc., (ch. 1, sc. in next sc.)

Times	39	39	41	42	43

Ch. 1, turn.

2nd row

Work in pattern across. Ch. 1, turn.

3rd row

Decreasing 1 ch.-1 sp. at both ends of row, work in pattern across. Ch. 1, turn.

4th row

Decreasing 1 sc. at both ends of row, work in pattern across. Ch. 1, turn. Work without decreasing for

Rows	0	2	2	2	2

Next row

Repeat 3rd row.

Following row

Repeat 4th row. Repeat last 4 rows 0 (0 : 0 : 2 : 2) times.

Next row

Decreasing 1 ch.-1 sp., at both ends of row, work in pattern across. Ch. 1, turn.

Following row

Decreasing 1 sc. at both ends of row, work in pattern across. Ch. 1, turn. Repeat last 2 rows until there remain on row

Sc.	14	14	14	17	17

Break off and fasten.

Left Front Raglan Armhole Shaping

1st row

With right side facing, skip next 4 sc. on last long row worked before armhole shaping, attach yarn to next sc., ch. 1, sc. in same sc., (ch. 1, sc. in next sc.)

Times   19   20   21   23   24

Ch. 1, turn.

2nd row

Work in pattern across. Ch. 1, turn.

3rd row

Decreasing 1 ch.-1 sp. at armhole edge, work in pattern across. Ch. 1, turn.

4th row

Work in pattern across, decreasing 1 sc. at armhole edge. Ch. 1, turn. Continue to shape armhole as for Right Front, reversing shaping until there remain on row, ending at front edge

Sc.   13   14   14   18   18

Do not ch. 1 at end of last row. Turn.

Neck Shaping

1st row

Sl. st. in first sc., (sl. st. in next ch.-1 and following sc.)

Times   3   4   4   6   6

ch. 1, * sc. in next sc., ch. 1. Repeat from * across, decreasing 1 sc. over last 2 sc. Ch. 1, turn.

2nd row

Decreasing 1 ch.-1 sp. at both ends of row, work in pattern across. Ch. 1, turn.

3rd row

Decreasing 1 sc. at both ends of row, work in pattern across. Ch. 1, turn. Repeat last 2 rows until 4 sc. remain. Keeping neck edge straight, continue to shape armhole as before until 1 sc. remains.
Break off and fasten.

Sleeves

Starting at lower edge with Size H hook, (having 9 ch. to 2 inches) make a chain of

Stitches	52	52	56	56	60
Work in pattern as for Body for					
Rows	10	10	12	12	12
having on each row					
Sc.	26	26	28	28	30

Next row

Make 2 sc. in first sc.—**1 sc. increased**; ch. 1, * sc. in next sc., ch. 1. Repeat from * across, ending with 2 sc. in last sc.—another sc. increased. Ch. 1, turn.

Following row

Sc. in first sc., ch. 1, * sc. in next sc., ch. 1. Repeat from * across to within last 2 sc., sc. in next sc., ch. 1, sc. in last sc.—1 ch.-1 sp. increased at both ends of row. Work without increasing for

Rows	10	10	12	12	12
Repeat last					
Rows	12	12	14	14	14
until there are on row					
Sc	32	32	34	34	36
Work without increasing until total length is					
Inches	13	13½	14	14	14½

Top Shaping

1st row

(Sl. st. in next sc. and in following ch.) twice; ch. 1, * sc. in next sc. Ch. 1.
Repeat from * across to within last 3 sc., sc. in next sc.
Ch. 1, turn.

2nd row

Work across in pattern. Ch. 1, turn. Starting with 3rd row, work same as for Back Raglan Armhole Shapings until there remain on row

Sc.				
2	2	2	4	4

Break off and fasten.

SCARF

Starting at narrow edge with Size H hook, ch. 22. Work in pattern as for Body until length is 4½ inches, having 11 sc. on each row.

Next row

Work in pattern across, decreasing the 2nd and next-to-the-last ch.-1 sp. Ch. 1, turn.

Following row

Work in pattern across, decreasing the 2nd and next-to-last sc. Ch. 1, turn. Work 2 rows even, Repeat last 4 rows until 7 sc. and 6 ch.-1 sps. remain on row. Work even until total length is 31 inches.

Next row

Sc. in first sc., ch. 1, 2 sc. in next sc., ch. 1, * sc. in next sc., ch. 1. Repeat from * across to within last 2 sc., 2 sc. in next sc., ch. 1, sc. in next sc. Ch. 1, turn.

Following row

Sc. in first sc., * ch. 1, sc. in next sc. Repeat from * across—2 ch.-1 sps. increased on row. Ch. 1, turn. Work 2 rows even. Repeat last 4 rows until there are 11 sc. and 10 ch.-1 sps. on row. Work even until total length is 38 inches. Do not ch. 1 at end of last row. Turn. Being careful to keep work flat, work sc. around entire outer edge of Scarf, making 3 sc. in same place at each corner. Join with sl. st. to first sc. Break off and fasten.

Block to measurements. Sew sleeve seams. Sew in sleeves.

EDGING

1st row

With Size H hook and right side of Coat facing, work 1 row of sc. around neck edge, holding in to fit. Ch. 1, turn.

2nd row

Sc. in each sc. around. Turn.

3rd row

Sl. st. in each sc. around. Do not turn. Being careful to keep work flat, sc. evenly along left front edge, lower edge and right front edge, making 3 sc. in same place at each corner. Join to first sl. st. Break off and fasten. Work 1 round of sc. evenly along each sleeve edge. Find center of scarf and place a marker 3 inches away from center at one long edge. With wrong side of scarf edging facing and having marker meet center of coat neck, sew scarf around neck edge, leaving 1½ inches free from each front edge. Sew large hook and eye to neck corners. Fold scarf and tie as shown.

SUGGESTED COLORS
Light Gold
Dark Camel
Cardinal
Dark Green
Dark Purple
Staccato Blue

How to make an Evening Shawl

Materials

Heart Super Fingering, 3 Ply (1 oz. skeins): 11 ounces; Steel Hook No. 1/0 (zero).

Measurements
36 ins. square without fringe.
Fringe 9 ins. in length.

Gauge
Each joined Motif = 6 inches square.

Actual st. for Evening Shawl

Method

First motif

Begin by making 5 ch.

1st row

Leaving the last loop of each on hook, work 2 tr. into the 5th ch. from hook, (3 loops on hook) y.o.h. and draw through all loops on hook (1 hlf. grp. made) 4 ch., leaving the last loop of each on hook, 3 tr. into the same st. (4 loops on hook) y.o.h. and draw through all loops on hook. (1 grp. made.) Turn.

2nd row

4 ch. (this forms the 1st tr. of 1 hlf. grp.) and 2 more tr. into top of 1st hlf. grp., 4 ch., 3 tr into same st. (these 3 tr., 4 ch., and 3 tr. form 1 grp.) Skip 4 ch., 1 grp. into top of next hlf. grp. Turn (2 grps.)

3rd row

4 ch., 1 grp. into top of 1st hlf. grp., skip 4 ch., 1 grp. into top of next hlf. grp. (this gives a complete grp. between the grps. of last row) skip 4 ch., 1 grp. into top of next hlf. grp. Turn (3 grps.)
Work as for 3rd row, 2 times more, inc. 1 grp. on each row (5 grps.) Turn.

6th row

4 ch., 1 hlf. grp. into top of 1st hlf. grp. * skip 4 ch., 1 grp. into top of next hlf. grp.
Repeat from * across ending with skip 4 ch., 1 hlf. grp. into top of last hlf. grp. Turn.

Work 4 more rows in the same way as 6th row. End last row with 2 hlf. grps.

1st round

Work around motif with 5 sc. into each row end for 5 rows, 1 sc. between rows, 5 sc. into each of the next 5 row ends, 1 sc. between 2 hlf. grps. at beg. of motif. 5 sc. into each of the next 5 row ends, 1 sc. between rows, 5 sc. into each of next 5 row ends. 1 sc. between hlf. grps. (Block to form a 4 in. square.)

2nd round

Sl. st. to 2nd sc., 1 ch., sc. in next sc., * 5 ch., skip 4 sc., 1 sc. into next sc.

Repeat from * 3 times, 5 ch., skip 2 sc., 1 sc. into next sc. (between grps.), 5 ch., skip 2 sc. 1 sc. into next sc. (corner); 5 ch. skip 4 sc., 1 sc. into next sc. Work all around square in this way, ending last corner with 5 ch., sl. st. into 1st sc.

(There will now be 4—5 ch. grps. on each side of motif and 2—5 ch. grps. at each corner.)

3rd round

Sl. st. to 3rd ch. 1 ch., 1 sc. into same ch. * (7 ch. sl. st. into 4 ch. from hook, 3 ch., 1 sc. into center ch. of next 5 ch.) 3 times; 7 ch. sl. st. into 4 ch. from hook, 3 ch., 4 dc. into next corner 5 ch. loop. 7 ch., sl. st. into 4 ch. from hook, 3 ch. 4 dc. into next corner 5 ch. loop. 7 ch. sl. st. into 4 ch. from hook, 3 ch., 1 sc. into center ch. of next 5 ch.

Repeat from * all around. Sl. st. into 1st sc. Fasten-off.

Second Motif

Work as for 1st motif until 2nd round has been worked. Work 3rd round up to 1st corner, then work thus—4 dc. into 1st corner 5 ch. loop, 7 ch. (keeping patterns matching). Join to corner loop of 1st motif with a sl. st., 3 ch. Turn. Skip 3 ch. sl. st. into next ch., 3 ch., 4 dc. into next 5 ch. loop of 2nd motif. 7 ch. sl. st. into next loop of 1st motif, 3 ch. Turn, skip 3 ch., sl. st. into next ch. * 3 ch., 1 sc. into center of next 5 ch. loop on 2nd motif, 7 ch. sl. st. into next loop of 1st motif 3 ch., turn, skip 3 ch. sl. st., into next ch.

Repeat from * 3 times, 3 ch., 4 dc. into next 5 ch. loop of 2nd motif, 7 ch., join to 2nd corner loop of 1st motif with a sl. st., 3 ch. Turn. Skip 3 ch., sl. st. into next ch., 3 ch. 4 dc., into next 5 ch. loop of 2nd motif, continue all around as for 1st motif. Make 6 X 6 motifs in same way, joining motifs as 2nd motif was joined to 1st motif (where 4 corners meet join corners to previously joined corners).

Fringe

Method

Cut strands of yarn 19 ins. in length (or whatever length is desired). Knot 6-8 strands into each loop around shawl. Cut ends of fringe evenly all around. Press shawl very lightly over a slightly damp cloth.

SUGGESTED COLORS
Glacier Green
Periwinkle
White
Black
Mulberry
Village Blue

How to make
Gold Slippers

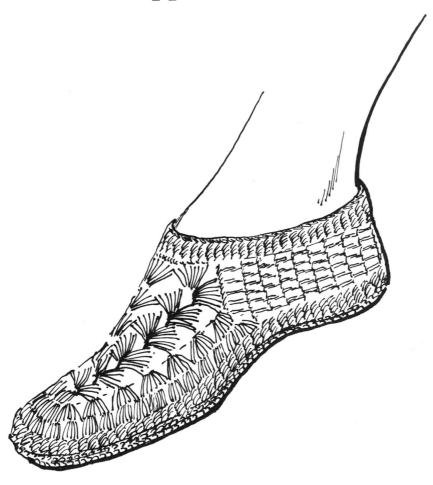

Materials

Metallic "Knit-Cro-Sheen": 2 balls of Gold and **"Speed-Cro-Sheen" Mercerized Cotton**: 2 balls of Black; Steel
Hook No. 4; 1 pair of inner soles; ¾ yard round elastic. For Sole—6 sc. make 1 inch; 6 rounds make 1 inch.
Directions are written for Small Size. Changes for Medium and Large sizes are in parentheses.

Method

SOLE

(Make 2) Starting at center with "Speed-Cro-Sheen" ch. 32 (38 : 44).

1st round
3 sc. in 2nd ch. from hook, sc. in 15 (18 : 21) ch., dc. in 14 (17 · 20) ch., 7 dc. in last ch. (toe); working along opposite side of starting chain, make dc. in 14 (17 : 20) ch., sc. in 15 (18 : 21) ch., 2 sc. in same place as first 3 sc. were made. *Do not join.*

2nd round
Sc. in each st. around, increasing 5 sc. evenly spaced across heel and 7 sc. evenly spaced across toe—*to inc. 1 sc., make 2 sc. in 1 st.* Repeat 2nd round until 6 (6 : 7) rounds have been completed. At end of last round sl. st. in next sc.
Break off.
Insert inner sole between sole pieces and, working through both thicknesses, sc. closely around edges.

INSTEP

Starting at toe end, with Gold, ch. 10.

1st row
In 5th ch. from hook make 2 dc., ch. 2 and 2 dc. (shell made), skip 2 ch., make a shell in next ch., skip next ch., dc. in next ch. Ch. 4, turn.

2nd row
(In sp. of next shell make 2 dc., ch. 3 and 2 dc.—shell over shell made) twice; dc. in top of turning chain. Ch. 4, turn.

3rd row
(In sp. of next shell make 3 dc., ch. 2 and 3 dc.) twice; dc. in top of turning chain. Ch. 4, turn.

4th, 5th and 6th rows
Work as for previous rows, making 3 dc., ch. 3 and 3 dc. shells on *4th row*; 4 dc., ch. 2 and 4 dc. shells on *5th row*, and 4 dc., ch. 3 and 4 dc. shells on *6th row*. Ch. 4 at end of last row but do not turn.

Now work around instep piece.
1st row
Make 4 dc. in first 6 sps. on side, 2 dc. at base of next shell, 2 dc. in each of next 2 ch., 2 dc. at base of next shell, 4 dc. in last 6 sps. on side.

SIDE PIECE

1st row
Dc. over bar of last dc. made, ch. 1, dc. in same sp. as the last 4-dc. group was made, (ch. 1, skip 1 dc. of shell, dc. in next dc.) twice; ch. 1, dc. in shell sp. (5 sps.). Ch. 4, turn.

2nd and 3rd rows
(Dc. in next sp., ch. 1) 4 times; dc. in 3rd ch. of turning chain (5 sps.). Ch. 4, turn.

4th row
In first sp. make (dc., ch. 1) twice (1 sp. increased at inner edge); (dc. in next sp., ch. 1) 3 times; dc. in 3rd ch. of turning chain. Ch. 4, turn.

5th row

Work without increasing. Repeat last 2 rows until there are 10 rows in all (9 sps. on last row). Work even until side piece measures without stretching 5½ (6½ : 7½)-ins. Break off.

Attach thread to top of first dc. of 4-dc. group on other side, ch. 4, dc. in next loop, ch. 1, dc. in same sp. as 4-dc. group was made, (ch. 1, skip 1 dc. of shell, dc. in next dc.) twice; ch. 1, dc. in shell sp. Ch. 4, turn.

Complete side piece to correspond with other side.

Work around lower edge as follows:

1st row

Work right side of the row across instep facing, attach thread to side of last sp. at heel end, ch. 3, 4 dc. in end of each row across side piece, dc. in each dc. across toe end; 4 dc. in end of each row on side. Ch. 1, turn.

2nd row

Sc. in each dc. across. Break off. Sew back seam. Work around top edge.

1st round

Attach thread at back seam, ch. 4, in end of each row on side piece make (dc., ch. 1) twice; (dc. in dc. of shell, ch. 1) 9 times; in end of each row make (dc., ch. 1) twice. Join with sl. st. to 3rd ch. of ch.-4.

2nd round

Working over elastic, sc. in each dc. and ch. around. Join and break off.

Draw elastic in to fit and sew ends securely. Sew top to sole. Make other slipper the same way.

How to make a Blazer

Materials

Red Heart Knitting Worsted, 4 Ply:

SIZES

	6	8	10	12	14	16
WHITE						
Ounces	16	18	20	22	24	26
GERANIUM						
Ounces	2	2	2	2	3	3

Plastic or Bone Hook Size J
8 Buttons

BLOCKING MEASUREMENTS

SIZES	6	8	10	12	14	16
Body Chest Size (In Inches)	30½	31½	32½	34	36	38
Actual Crocheting Measurements						
Bust (buttoned)	32	34	36	38	40	42
Width across back at underarm	16	17	18	19	20	21
Width across back above armhole shaping	13	13½	14	15	15½	16
Width across each front at underarm (excluding border)	10	10¾	11¼	12	12¾	13¼
Length of side seam	11½	12	12½	13	13½	13½
Length from shoulder to lower edge	18	19	20	21	22	22½
Length of sleeve seam	10	11½	13	14	14½	15
Width across sleeve at upper arm	12½	13	13½	14	14½	15

Gauge
3 sc. = 1 inch; 4 rows = 1 inch.

Method

Starting at lower edge with White, ch.

Stitches	45	48	51	54	57	60

(3 ch. = 1 inch)

1st row (right side)
Sc. in 2nd ch. from hook and in each ch. across.
There are

Stitches	44	47	50	53	56	59

Ch. 1, turn.

2nd row
Sc. in each sc. across. Ch. 1, turn. Drop White, attach Red.

Next 2 rows
With Red repeat 2nd row. Change colors.

Following 4 rows
With White repeat 2nd row. At end of 8th row drop White, attach Red.

9th row
Working over the unused color to conceal it work color pattern as follows: * With Red sc. in next sc., with White sc. in next sc. Repeat from * across. **For sizes 10, 14 and 18** end with a Red sc. Break off Red and fasten.

Next 4 rows
With White repeat 2nd row.

14th and 15th rows
With Red repeat 2nd row. Break off Red and fasten.

Remainder of Back is worked with White only. Repeat 2nd row until total length is 8 inches.

Next row
2 sc. in first sc.—**1 sc. increased**, sc. in each sc. across, increasing 1 sc. in last sc. Work even for 2 inches, then inc. 1 sc. at both ends of next row.

There are
Stitches | 48 | 51 | 54 | 57 | 60 | 63

There are Stitches	48	51	54	57	60	63
Work even until total length is Inches	11½	12	12½	13	13½	13½

ending with a wrong-side row. **Omit turning chain at end of last row.**
Turn.

Armhole Shaping

1st row
Sl. st. in next

Stitches	3	3	3	3	4	4

Ch. 1, sc. in next sc. and in each sc. across to within last

Stitches	3	3	3	3	4	4

Do not work in these last sts. Ch. 1, turn.

2nd row
Sc. in each sc. across. Ch. 1, turn.

3rd row
*Draw up a loop in each of next 2 sc., yarn over and draw through all 3 loops on hook—***1 sc. decreased**, sc. in each sc. across to within last 2 sc., dec. 1 sc. Ch. 1, turn. **Repeat** last 2 rows

Times	1	1	2	2	2	2

Work even on

Stitches	38	41	42	45	46	49

until length from first row of armhole shaping is

Inches	6½	7	7½	8	8½	9

Shoulder Shaping

1st row
Sl. st. in next 3 sts. (3 sts. bound-off at beg. of row), ch. 1, sc. in next st. and in each st. across to within last 3 sts. **Do not work in these last 3 sts.,** (3 sts. bound-off at end of row). Ch. 1, turn. Repeat last row

Times	2	3	2	2	2	4

For Sizes 8, 12, 14, and 16 only
Bind off at each end of next row

Stitches	2	0	4	5	5	0

Break off and fasten. Remaining sts. are for back of neck.

Left Front

With White, ch.

Stitches	29	31	33	35	37	39

1st row
Sc. in 2nd ch. from hook and in each ch. across. There are

Stitches	28	30	32	34	36	38

Work as for Back until total length is 8 inches, ending with a wrong-side row.

Next row
Starting at **side edge**, inc. one st. in first sc., work across. Work even for 2 inches. On next row inc. one st. at side edge. Work even on

Stitches	30	32	34	36	38	40

until total length is same as Back to armhole shaping, ending at side edge. Turn.

Armhole Shaping

1st row
Sl. st. in first

Stitches	3	3	3	3	4	4

Ch. 1, sc. in next sc. and in each sc. across. Ch. 1, turn. Dec. one st. at armhole edge every other row

Times	2	2	3	3	3	3

Work even on

Stitches	25	27	28	30	31	33

until length from first row of armhole shaping is

Inches	3	3½	4	4	4½	4½

ending at front edge.

Neck Shaping

1st row

Draw up a loop in first 3 sc., yarn over and draw through all loops on hook—**2 sc. decreased**, sc. in each sc. across. Ch. 1, turn.

2nd row

Sc. in each sc. across to within last 3 sc., dec. 2 sc. Then dec. one st. at same edge on every row until there remain

Stitches	11	12	13	14	14	15

Work even until length from first row of armhole shaping is same as Back to shoulder shaping, ending at side edge.

Shoulder Shaping

1st row

Sl. st. in next 3 sc., ch. 1, sc. in each sc. across. Ch. 1, turn.

2nd row

Sc. in each sc. across to within last 3 sc. Ch. 1, turn.

3rd row

Repeat first row.

For Size 18 only

4th row

Repeat 2nd row. Break off and fasten.

With pins mark the position of 4 buttons evenly spaced on front edge, having the first pin 2 inches up from lower edge and the last pin ½ inch down from first row of neck shaping.

Right Front

Work as for Left Front for 2 inches ending with a wrong-side row. Ch. 1, turn.

Next row

Starting at front edge, sc. in first sc., ch. 1 for buttonhole, skip next sc., sc. in next

| Stitches | 8 | 8 | 10 | 12 | 12 | 16 |

Ch. 1, skip next sc., sc. in each remaining sc. Ch. 1, turn.

Following row

Sc. in each sc. and each ch.-1 sp. across—**a set of buttonholes made.** Ch. 1, turn. Continue as for Left Front, reversing shapings and making 3 more sets of buttonholes to correspond with pins.

Sleeves

Starting at lower edge, with Red, ch.

| Stitches | 24 | 26 | 26 | 27 | 29 | 30 |

1st and 2nd rows

Repeat first and 2nd rows of Back. There are

| Stitches | 23 | 25 | 25 | 26 | 28 | 29 |

At end of 2nd row, break off Red, attach White. With White only repeat 2nd row of Back for pattern. Work in pattern, increasing one st. at both ends of row, every

| Inches | 1¼ | 1¼ | 1½ | 1½ | 1½ | 1½ |
| Times | 7 | 7 | 8 | 8 | 8 | 8 |

Work even on these

| Stitches | 37 | 39 | 41 | 42 | 44 | 45 |

until total length is

| Inches | 10 | 11½ | 13 | 14 | 14½ | 15 |

Top Shaping

1st row

Repeat first row of Armhole Shaping of Back. Dec. one st. at both ends of every other row until there remain

| Stitches | 17 | 17 | 17 | 16 | 16 | 17 |

Dec. 2 sts. at both ends of next 3 rows. Break off and fasten.

Making-up

Block to measurements. Sew side, shoulder and sleeve seams. Sew in sleeves.

Edging

1st row

With right side facing, attach White to lower front edge. Being careful to keep work flat, sc. along front edge, making 3 sc. in end sc. on first row of neck shaping, sc. around neck edge, decreasing one st at each shoulder seam, then work along left front edge to correspond. Break off and fasten.

2nd row

With wrong side facing, attach Red to last White sc made and work along front edges and neck edge same as previous row. Ch. 1, turn.

3rd row

Work as for previous row.
Turn.

4th row

Sl. st. in each sc. across. Break off and fasten. Make buttonhole stitch around buttonholes. Sew on buttons.

SUGGESTED COLORS
Bisque and Coffee
Baby Yellow and Rust
Light Blue and Cobalt
Nile Green and Emerald

How to make a Cape

Materials

Materials

Super Fingering, 3 Ply (1 oz. skeins): 4 skeins of White; Steel Hooks No. 1/0 (zero) and No. 8; 1 yard of any color tubular jersey, 54 inches wide.
Mercerized Sewing Thread: 1 spool of matching color.

ROSE

(Make 17) Starting at center with No. 1/0 hook, ch. 5. Join with sl. st. to form ring.

1st round
Ch. 1, 12 sc. in ring. Join to first sc.

2nd round
Ch. 1, sc. in joining, (ch. 3, sc. in next sc.) 11 times; ch. 3. Join to first sc.—12 loops.

3rd round
In each loop around make sc., hlf. dc., 3 dc., hlf. dc. and sc.—**petal made.** Join—12 petals.

4th round
Ch. 1, holding petals forward throughout, make an sc. around bar of sc. used for joining of 2nd round, * ch. 3, (sc. around bar of next sc. of 2nd round) twice. Repeat from * around, ending with ch. 3, sc. around bar of last sc. of 2nd round. Join—6 loops.

5th round
Repeat 3rd round. Join—6 petals.

6th round
Ch. 2, holding petals forward throughout, * from back of work sc. around bar of center dc. of next petal, ch. 4. Repeat from * around. Join to first sc.

7th round
Repeat 5th round

8th round
Work as for 6th round making ch. 5 instead of ch. 4.

9th round
In each loop around make sc. h. dc., 3 dc., ch. 3, 3 dc., h. dc. and sc. Join.

10th round
Sl. st. in top of each st. to center loop of first petal; ch. 1, sc. in next ch.-3 loop of same petal, * ch. 5, (in sc. just made make dc., ch. 1 and dc.—**shell made**; ch. 1, turn; sc. in ch.-1 sp. of last shell made, ch. 5, turn) twice; make a shell in sc. just made, sc. in ch.-3 loop of next petal. Repeat from * around. Join—18 shells. Break off and fasten.

Making-up

Cut open one fold of the tubular jersey, then fold piece in half crosswise, having a piece of double thickness 18 inches wide by 54 inches long. Round off one corner at each end from raw edge to fold edge. Make a ¼ inch hem along one raw edge and baste (this is right side of stole). Make a ⅜ inch hem along other raw edge and baste (this is wrong side). Slipstitch fold line of ⅜ inch hem to hem of right side, having right side extending ⅛ inch.

EDGING

With right side of stole facing and No. 8 hook, attach yarn to beg. of extending edge.

1st row

Ch. 1, sc. evenly along entire extending edge, having a number of sc. divisible by 4, plus 1. Ch. 1, turn. Change to No. 1/0 hook.

2nd row

Sc. in first sc., * ch. 3, skip next 3 sc., sc. in next sc. Repeat from * across. Ch. 1, turn.

3rd row

Sc. in first loop, * ch. 5, in last sc. made make (dc., ch. 1) twice; sc. in next loop. Repeat from * across, ending with ch. 1, sl. st. in last sc. Break off and fasten. Press. Having roses evenly spaced along entire curved edge as shown, sew center and outer edge of each rose to stole.

How to make an Overblouse

Materials

Super Fingering, 3 Ply (1 oz. skeins): 9 (10 : 11) skeins of Peppermint.
For Sizes 12 and 16, use Crochet Hook Size E.
For Sizes 14 use Steel Hook No. 1.

Gauge
For Size 12, Motif measures 4⅝ inches square.
For Size 14, Motif measures 4 inches square.
For Size 16, Motif measures 3½ inches square.

BLOCKING MEASUREMENTS

SIZES	12	14	16
Body Bust Size (In Inches)	34	36	38

ACTUAL CROCHETING MEASUREMENTS

	12	14	16
Bust	37	40	42
Width across back or front at underarm	18½	20	21
Length from back of neck to lower edge	18½	20	21

Directions are given for Size 12. Changes for Sizes 14 and 16 are in parentheses.

First Motif

Starting at center, ch. 8. Join with a sl. st. to form ring.

1st round
Ch. 1, 18 sc. in ring. Join to first sc.

2nd round
Ch. 1, sc. in joining, ch. 5, (skip 2 sc., sc. in next sc., ch. 5) 5 times. Join to first sc.—6 loops.

3rd round
Ch. 1, in each loop make sc., hlf. dc., 5 dc., hlf. dc. and sc.—6 petals.

4th round
Ch. 1, * holding petal forward and working behind the petal, sc. around the bar of next sc. made 2 rounds below, ch. 7. Repeat from * around. Join—6 loops.

5th round
In each loop make sc., hlf. dc., dc., 7 tr., dc., hlf. dc. and sc.

6th round
Repeat 4th round.

7th round
Sl. st. in first loop, ch. 3, 7 dc. in same loop, * 8 dc. in next loop. Repeat from * around. Join to top of ch. 3. Counting the ch. 3 as 1 dc., there are 48 dc. on round.

8th round
Ch. 3, * tr. in next 2 dc., ch. 4, sl. st. in 4th ch. from hook—**picot made**; tr. in next 2 dc., dc. in next dc., (ch. 2, dc. in next 3 dc.) twice; ch. 2, dc. in next dc. **Repeat** from * around, ending with dc. in last 3 dc., hlf. dc. in top of ch.-3 to form last sp.

9th round
Ch. 1, sc. in sp. just formed, * (*ch. 5, sl. st. in 4th ch. from hook*) *twice and ch 1*—**picot loop made**; in next picot make sc., picot loop and sc. for corner picot loop, (make picot loop, skip 3 sts., sc. in next ch.-2 sp.) 3 times. Repeat from * around, ending with 3 picot loops following last corner. Join.

For Size 16 only
Break off and fasten at end of last round—20 picot loops.

For Sizes 12 and 14 Only

10th round
Sl. st. in first 2 ch., ch. 1, sc. between the picots of same picot loops, * make a picot loop, sc. between picots in next picot loop. Making a corner picot loop in each corner picot loop, repeat from * around. Join. Break off and fasten.

Second Motif

Work as for First Motif until 9 (9 : 8) rounds have been completed.
For Sizes 12 and 14 only

Next round
Sl. st. in first 2 ch., ch. 1, sc. between the picots of same picot loop, make a picot loop, sc. in corner picot loop, ch. 1, picot; with wrong side of First Motif facing, sl. st. in any corner picot loop on First Motif between picots, make a picot, ch. 1, sc. in same corner picot loop on Second Motif, * ch. 1, picot, sl. st. in corresponding loop on First Motif, picot, ch. 1, sc. in next loop on Second Motif. Repeat from * across, joining next corner picot loop to corner loop on First Motif. Now starting at * on 10th round on First Motif, complete the round.

For Size 16 only

Next round
Ch. 1, sc. in sp. just formed, make picot loop, sc. in next picot, ch. 1, picot; with wrong side of First Motif facing, sl. st. in any corner picot loop on First Motif between picots, make a picot, ch. 1, sc. in same corner picot on Second Motif, (ch. 1, picot, sl. st. in corresponding loop on First Motif, picot, ch. 1, sc. in next ch.-2 sp. on Second Motif) 3 times; ch. 1, picot, sl. st. in next loop on First Motif, picot, ch. 1, sc. in next corner picot on Second Motif, ch. 1, picot, sl. st. in next corner loop on First Motif, picot, ch. 1, sc. in same corner picot on Second Motif, (make picot loop, sc. in next ch.-2 sp. on Second Motif) 3 times. Now starting at * on 9th round on First Motif, complete the round.

Back

Make 4 (5, 6) rows of 4 (5, 6) motifs, joining motifs as Second Motif was joined to First Motif (where corners meet, join corner loops to previous joinings).

Front

Work same as Back.

Sleeve

(Make 2) **For Sizes 12 and 14 only**
Make 3 motifs as for Motif on Size 12, joining one side of the Second Motif to the first side of the First Motif, and one side of the Third Motif to Second Motif and opposite side to the third side of the First Motif.

For Size 16 only
Make 4 motifs as for Motif on Size 16, joining one side of Second Motif to the first side of First Motif; one side of Third Motif to Second Motif; one side of Fourth Motif to Third Motif and opposite side of Fourth Motif to third side of First Motif.

Making-up

Block to measurements. Holding Front and Back together, sew a 4 (4½ : 5)-inch seam at both ends of top edges, leaving 10½ (11 : 11) inches free at center for neck edge. Starting at lower edge, sew 12 (13¼ : 13¾)-inch side seams, leaving 6½ (6¾ : 7¼) inches of side edges free for armholes. Sew in sleeves, having center of one motif meet the shoulder seam.

SUGGESTED COLORS
White
Light Yellow
Blue Jewel
Peppermint

LENGTHENING THE GARMENTS

Current fashion trends allow us to wear whatever length of skirt we fancy. However, just in case the future vogue decrees that skirts must get longer, I am giving here 4 ways by which the garment in this book can be lengthened without too much misery.1

Method 1
See pattern 1. (Reading Patterns.) This is very effective for a garment worked in plain fabric.

Method 2
To lengthen an open pattern stitch design—work a border of sc. round the lower edge of dress or skirt for 1—1½ ins., then 1 inch of the pattern stitch of the garment.

Method 3
Lengthen the skirt at the waistline.
Finish with 1 row of 1 sc., into each st. Fasten-off.

Method 4
This is perhaps the easiest. When starting a dress or skirt, if it is worked in a close stitch pattern make the finished length 2—2½ ins. longer than specified in the pattern. Turn up 'a hem, taking care that the rows are perfectly even all the way round. Work 2 rows sc. as a border round lower edge or—with the Right side facing, 1 row dc. Then with the wrong side facing work 1 sl. st. into each sc. Fasten-off. Blind st. hem to skirt.

When you want to lengthen your skirt all you have to do is take out the border and let down the hem. Press hemline out, using a damp cloth, a hot iron and a very light hand.

Method 2
(lower edge)

LINING FOR CROCHET GARMENTS

It is not essential to line a crochet garment especially if it is worked in a close fabric. Some people, though, may prefer to anyway. Skirts, I think, feel nicer to wear when lined although an unlined crochet skirt will neither 'sit out' nor go baggy at the knees.

Materials for lining

This again is a matter of personal taste but, as a crochet garment is long-lasting and stands up to a lot of hard wear, I prefer to use a good quality silk. Rayon or synthetic fabrics also make nice linings.

Lining a skirt

You will need 1½ yds. of 36 ins. wide material for an average length skirt. Cut out the lining before joining your skirt together.

Method

Iron out any creases there are in the material and fold in half with selvages meeting evenly. Lay 1 piece of the skirt on the lining, placing pins all around to prevent movement. Cut lining 1½ ins. wider than fabric at side edges up to hip line then 2½ ins wider than fabrics up to waist line (this is to ensure that the lining will pull over the hips when putting skirt on) 2 ins. longer at lower edge and omit turning at the waist.

With right sides of lining together, join side edges leaving 7 ins. from lower edge open (this is for walking purposes). Press seams open. At lower edge, fold back the 7 ins. and make a hem. Strengthen the top of the opening with a machine stitch across. Turn up the lower edge of Back and Front for 2 ins., and hem. Press all the seams. Turn in 1 inch at the waist and place pins at Center Front and Back. With wrong side of lining facing wrong side of skirt, pin together as close as possible under the lower part of the waist elastic, at side seams, Center Front and Back and at intervals in between, distributing the fulness evenly. Sew with a strand of wool.

Lining a coat

Method

Cut lining out before joining coat together. Iron out any creases there are in the material. Place coat pieces on lining and pin round the edges to prevent movement.

Back of Coat

Cut lining 1½ ins. wider than fabric all round 1 inch is for turnings and the extra inch (½ inch each side) is for the pleat at the back of neck.

Front and Sleeves

Cut lining 1 inch wider all round for turnings. Sew shoulder and side seams together, and sew sleeve seams and sew sleeves into lining. With wrong side of lining facing wrong side of coat, pin lining to coat. Make a small pleat at the back of neck and sew with a herringbone stitch for about 3 ins. down. Turn in turnings of lining and sew to coat. Turn up lining at ends of sleeves and sew to coat. Turn up lower edge and hem. Catch lining at side seams of coat.

CARE OF CROCHET GARMENTS

When you have crocheted one of these garments and know what a joy it is to wear—do take care of it! It won't need much attention and there is no question of it always demanding to be pressed. Crocheted garments don't crush—one can wear them all day and look just as fresh and elegant at the end as at the beginning.

When not in use keep the garment folded neatly in a drawer or on a shelf in the wardrobe. (Not hanging please.)

Don't allow your suit to become too soiled before having it either cleaned or washed. I must confess that I, myself, like to have mine cleaned at least twice before washing, I really believe that this is just a whim because I am still wearing a suit I made 10 years ago which has had innumerable washings.

Washing crocheted garments is very simple really. Do use mild soap flakes. Wash by hand, squeezing in warm water and rinse thoroughly, also in warm water until water is quite clear. Squeeze as much water out as possible and lay the garment on a dry towel until it is nearly dry. Finish-off by putting it on a hanger to dry.

Pressing after washing

Press lightly with a steam iron if available, if not use a damp cloth with a hot iron—but not too hot—and certainly with a very light hand.

INDEX

DATE DUE